GRIME & GLORY

*Tales of the Great Western
1892–1947*

ADRIAN VAUGHAN

John Murray

© Adrian Vaughan 1985

First published 1985
by John Murray (Publishers) Ltd
50 Albemarle Street, London WIX 4BD

Typeset by Inforum Ltd, Portsmouth
Printed and bound in Great Britain
by The Bath Press, Avon

British Library CIP Data
Vaughan, Adrian
Grime and glory : tales of the Great Western
1892–1947.
1. Great Western Railway—History
I. Title
385'.0942   HE3020.G8
ISBN 0–7195–4244–8

To Driver Charlie Turner
for all his patient help over the years;
to Jack Ody, Bert and Vi Bourton,
Ben Davies, Sid Tyler, Harry Keen,
and to the memory of the thousands of brave men
who served the Great Western's Iron Way
through years of peace and war,
this book is affectionately dedicated

CONTENTS

ILLUSTRATIONS

Between pages 84 and 85

ACKNOWLEDGEMENTS AND LIST OF SOURCES

This book would not have been possible without the generous help of many friends to whom I am delighted to acknowledge my debt: the staff of the Public Record Office, Kew, in the Reading Room, Cloakroom and Restaurant; the staff at the British Library, Colindale; the Archivist of the Signalling Record Society, David Collins; D.M. Allen, Divisional Librarian, Swindon, and Roger Trayhurn in the Reference Section there; the staff at Llanelli Library; Michael H.C. Baker, Frank Dumbleton and Fred Gray of the Great Western Society; Brian Searle and John Lucking; Ian Coulson and Christian Tagholm of Western Region HQ, Swindon, and Lenny Leane of Paddington; David Blagrove, for his recollections of Sir Felix Pole, incorporated in the Epilogue; Mrs Pamela Cummings, Jim Honey's daughter, for photographs and papers; Driver Bert Bourton and his wife Vi, Ben Davies, Jack Kinch, Jack Ody and, in particular, Charlie Turner, who has been a source of constant help over the years; W. MacDonald, ex-GWR Staff Photographer, retired Head of the Chief Civil Engineer's Photographic Department, Paddington, for his generous help with this book and for his friendship over many years; Mike Esau, C.R.L. Coles, Dr Jack Hollick, Oxford Publishing Co. Ltd, and John Edgington of the National Railway Museum, York, for kindly supplying more fine photographs than I could use. Thanks, also, to my friend Relief Signalman John Morris for drawing the diagram in Chapter 11 at very short notice and Russell Carter for the diagram in Appendix 1 – a quart into a pint pot I think! I should also like to thank my publishers for their unfailing kindness, my editor Duncan McAra, and John Gammons, Pamela Hargreaves, and Charlie Bateman in Publicity. Always ready to provide a welcome, hot meal at the end of a tiring day's research was my sister Frances Travers and my friends Paul and Sue Dye, Ron and Jo Price. Last of all, I must thank those who have most to endure from me, my wife Susan and my daughters Rebecca and Connie without whose willing co-operation I would not get to Norwich to catch the train to London. The research for this book was drawn mainly from official documents from the Great Western Railway's archive now housed at the Public Record Office, Kew; newspapers at Colindale; also consulted was 'Locomotive Working in the 19th Century' by A.L. Ahrons, *Railway Magazine*; *I Drove the Cheltenham Flyer* by J.W. Street (Nicholson & Watson, 1951); *Dunkirk and the Great Western* by Brown, Ashley, (GWR, 1945); *The Nine Days of Dunkirk* by D. Devine; and 'The Llanelli Riots 1911', a scholarly article by Deian Hopkin supplied by Llanelli Public Library.

ONE

Jim Street joins the Broad Gauge

At nine o'clock on the morning of 11 May 1891, a fifteen-year-old boy, tall and well built for his age, walked over Westbourne bridge and made his way to the far end, to a gate which gave access to a staircase down to the tracks and the brick- and stone-built engine shed of the Great Western Railway. The gate-keeper, Tommy James, saw the lad coming and adopted his usual defence in such circumstances. 'Clear orf – there ain't no vacancies,' he shouted, though whether this was so he had no idea, he just did not want to be bothered with inquiries and giving directions. Undaunted, the boy produced a letter addressed to Mr John Armstrong, Locomotive Superintendent of the Great Western's London Division, and asked to be allowed to deliver it. Tommy had to let him through and the boy had passed his first test – determination. The letter was from the London District Engineer of the Great Western, a friend of the boy's father, and it recommended the bearer, James William Street, as honest and intelligent and therefore suitable material for employment in the locomotive department.

Mr Armstrong read the letter, approved it and sent young Jim Street to find his Foreman, John Webb, who would see that the formal test of literacy would be applied. In the Foreman's office Jim was asked to read half a page from a Dickens novel kept specially for the purpose, took down some dictation from the same volume and did some mental arithmetic all to the satisfaction of Webb's clerk, whereupon he was told he could report for work as an engine cleaner the following Monday at

6 a.m., to be prepared for five days of twelve-hour shifts and a half-day on Saturday in return for wages of 5 shillings a week.

Jim arrived for work promptly, determined from the start that he was going to be the best cleaner and, eventually, the best engine driver on the Great Western – and Jim Street was a very determined boy. The shed yard was full of activity as men strolled or hurried about their jobs. There were the firelighters, who each carried from a central furnace on their shoulder a heavy iron scoop of blazing coal, scrambling up the side of a locomotive, one-handed, into the cab. There were the fire-droppers raking out engines' ashpans, clearing clinker and ash, a gang of boilersmiths working with high-pressure hoses and long, thin steel rods on a boiler with all the 'mudholes' and plugs removed, to scrape and flush away the accumulation of lime-scale and silt from within. A fitter climbed from the pits over which the engines stood, spanners and a hammer in hand having closed up the brasses of a slack big-end bearing or after adjusting the brakes. Coal heavers tumbled fuel onto engines' tenders and bunkers but the tracks were free of litter. Any stray knobs of coal were tossed by thrifty drivers onto their tenders to assist in keeping their recorded coal consumption low enough to claim the fuel bonus. No filthy cotton waste lay around in soggy bundles – it was all gathered up and burned in the furnace that dried the sand used in the engines' sand-boxes to prevent the driving wheels slipping on wet or greasy rails.

Within the shed, framed by the semicircular entrance arches, engines gleamed in the semi-darkness; out in the yard, attended by enginemen and cleaners, they stood magnificent in the morning light. There were a handful of broad gauge machines – a six-coupled goods engine and a pair of Gooch 'eight-footers' up from Exeter overnight and two broad gauge 'Flyers' being groomed for down expresses out of Paddington later that day – and standard gauge engines from Weymouth, Worcester, Wales and Wolverhampton. The engines from the Northern Division were noticeable for the deep red-brown colour of their frames, blue-green boilers with black and white lining surmounted by chimneys carrying copper caps that were rolled and rounded, not flared and sharp edged like their Swindon-built brethren – for the Northern Division engines were out of Wolverhampton works which did things in its own way. Curiously, Swindon works was run by men trained at Wolverhampton yet once such men were down in Wiltshire they produced engines with quite different personas: rich green boilers, lined in orange and black, and bright Indian-red frames so that the yard would have looked to an ignorant observer as containing the engines of three companies, one of which ran 7-ft-gauge locomotives.

Jim was directed to the Foreman of Cleaners, Charlie Weller, a little, one-eyed cockney with a fringe of white beard from ear to ear under his bowler hat as if the beard were string, tying the hat down. Charlie was a very gentle individual, fond of books, especially poetry and indeed he was a poet, his verses for seasonal occasions or just for the joy of writing being nailed frequently on Tommy James' gate for the amusement of everyone. He had joined the Great Western in 1838, aged twenty, and since then had fractured his skull twice in falls from engines, his ribs had been broken when he was squeezed between closing buffers and he lost his eye when a piece of red hot cinder flew into it as he was raking out a fire. Yet, in spite of every misfortune, he remained cheerful and at seventy-three 'Old Charlie' – friend of Brunel and Gooch almost from the very beginning – was the shed's living legend, regarded with affection by everyone.

Charlie issued Jim with his daily ration of cleaning stuff: 2 lb of cotton waste and half a pint of 'Blue Billy' cleaning oil (Mr Armstrong did not allow tallow to be used on paintwork because it contained an acid which was harmful). In the shed yard three boys were carefully grooming an already highly polished, broad gauge 'Single' to a state of immaculate perfection. In the early sun the blocky brass letters of its nameplate, *Prometheus*, curved and flashed over the big, brass axle-box. Rows of rivet heads twinkled, yellow smoke rolled off the glossy black, copper-capped chimney as the boys swarmed over the boiler and along the framing. Charlie called a fourth boy out from the pit beneath the engine and sent Jim down in his place, saying, 'Wet your ball of waste with water before you put oil on it and then make the inside of the frames and wheels and the machinery as clean as the outside – wheels and all. This is Charlie Hayes's engine for the 'Dutchman' and if he gets any dirt on his hands when he goes under to oil round he'll have something to say to you.'

The boys worked hard all day and every day, cleaning *Prometheus* and two other engines as part of a regular team of attendants on those particular machines. The cleaners were a bright, cheeky crowd though there were some without the necessary stamina for the daily grind and they found it hard going. Their ration of cleaning materials was barely sufficient, so unguarded cotton waste or oil vanished without trace amongst the po-faced crew. The boldest spirits found Mr Armstrong's topper irresistible and occasionally a well-aimed ball of oily waste would send it flying – and the culprit flying for cover along a well-chosen line of retreat even before the missile struck home. Armstrong had been a rugby forward in his younger days and could still make a good run but the bold spirit was quicker when capture would have meant dismissal and no one was ever caught. Safer targets were to be found among the weaker members of the cleaning gangs and an exhausted lad who went to sleep during the midday break was likely to be flushed into wakefulness by a jet of cold water from a hosepipe slipped quietly up his trouser leg and, if the perpetrators were certain boys, the victim would have to think himself lucky that they had used only cold water.

Jim was drafted to a newly constituted night shift and was promoted to cleaning the outside of tank engines – the 'Tunnel Mokers' – working the GWR's suburban services eastward from Paddington, through the tunnels of the Metropolitan and District Railways to Aldgate and Mansion House; westwards to Windsor, Henley and Reading; south to the LBSCR/SER/

LCD terminal at Victoria; south-west to Hammersmith via Shepherd's Bush and to Richmond, via the West London line and District Railway. Gradually he rose through the cleaners' hierarchy to become a polisher of express engine boilers and brasses and gathered information about the engines' machinery from the diverse characters who drove them and who gave their time to answer cleaner-lads' inquiries. There was no other way for a boy to learn sufficiently to pass the Inspector's examination when the time came for promotion to fireman.

The drivers had spent half a lifetime working in any weather on cabless locomotives and were obviously very tough men, either by natural good fortune in possessing a strong constitution or by sheer, dogged, determination if they did not. Jacob Scaplehorn, driver of the broad gauge 'Single' *Sultan*, had become a driver in 1870 and shortly afterwards three fingers of his right hand were crushed under the wheel of an engine while he was reaching out for an oil can from the pit. The injuries healed and he had so impressed the Company's doctor that he allowed him to continue as a driver with only a finger and thumb on his right hand. In 1887 he had been on the 'Tunnel Mokers' which passed their exhaust steam to their water tanks rather than allowing it to billow out into the tunnels. This worked well for a while, until the water in the tanks became so hot that it no longer condensed the incoming steam. At that stage it was the practice to stand the engine over a pit and run the water away into the drains. Scaplehorn did this one day in 1887 on Westbourne Park shed and, having given the hundreds of gallons of water a chance to flow away, he stepped down into the pit to examine his engine's machinery. Unfortunately, the drain was blocked with ashes and he stepped into twelve inches of scalding water which burnt his foot and, as he recoiled backwards, he hit his head on the engine's draw-gear. He was off work for five weeks and came back to promotion to 1st class work driving the Gooch 'Single' *Alma*. One freezing night, just before Christmas 1890, he was coming into Swindon with *Alma* on the 4.30 p.m. up from Plymouth when the broad gauge convertible engine No 16 *Charles Saunders* collided with his. Both engines' crews were badly knocked about in the glancing crash, Jacob suffering a dislocated shoulder, yet he was back at work in two weeks.

In 1893 Jim Street was regular cleaner on Charlie Birdseye's succession of standard gauge 'Singles' – 'Cobham' class Nos 162 and 165 and 'Queen' class 1117 and 1130 – and getting the top rate for a cleaner of 2s 6d a day. Charlie Birdseye was a Wolverhampton man who became a top link, 8 shillings a day man at Paddington in 1885. He was an 'ace' driver until 16 June 1892 when he had the misfortune to walk through the brick arch of Green Lane bridge just as the 5.43 a.m. Acton to Smithfield meat train was passing through. How it was that Charlie neither saw nor heard the train no one ever knew, least of all himself, but his momentary preoccupation cost him four broken ribs and a lacerated skull. His injuries healed and he was able to go back to express work but his health was destroyed and he aged rapidly in looks, posture and with a certain paralysis in his left hand. His great strength of character kept him going and in spite of his pains he took time to help Jim Street and other keen young men who wanted to master the intricacies of railway rules and locomotive mechanics. Jim remembered Charlie Birdseye throughout his own, long, life.

There were many memorable characters on shed: Bill Reading, driver of the Gooch 'Single' *Great Britain*, who started as a twelve-year-old 'crane boy' at Paddington in 1853 eventually to become Royal train driver. And Johnny Coleman who did not. Coleman started as a lad in 1853 inside Swindon factory, transferred to 'the Loco', became a fireman in 1860 at the age of twenty-two and grew into a heavyweight, brass-bound kind of man and a 'rough 'n' ready' kind of driver. He was a good mate, yet a somewhat 'devil-may-care' attitude could, when the mood was on him, turn him into a very heavy-handed driver making life hard both for his fireman and for the small boilers of those days which were only just big enough for the job, when used carefully. His engine in 1891 was the broad gauge 'Single'

Great Western with which he hauled the last broad gauge 'Cornishman' out of Paddington at 10.15 a.m. on 29 May 1892 – an engine he had run out of steam and water on practically level track more than once. In 1896 he was the driver of No 10, an experimental, compound expansion engine built in 1886 with 7ft 8in. driving wheels and rebuilt as a simple expansion engine with 7ft wheels in 1890. It was never a successful engine at the best of times and on 9 January 1896 Coleman was in trouble with it on a down express, west of Didcot, on a very slightly rising gradient in the teeth of a westerly gale. Steam pressure was low, water in the tender was low and was almost out of sight in the boiler gauge glass. He kept stubbornly on, unwilling to sacrifice his professional pride to an emergency stop to raise steam and equally unwilling to risk official displeasure at 'stopping for a blow-up'. The result was that the firebox crown ceased to be covered by water, the fusible plug melted, allowing the remaining contents of the boiler to escape into the firebox. The subsequent overheating of the boiler was such that, when they came to a stand at Challow, smoke was oozing out from beneath the shiny, green lagging plates and flames were licking out from beneath the brass dome where oxygen, reaching the baking, wooden lagging around the boiler, caused the wood to catch fire. Confusion, if not outright panic, ensued. The engine's bucket was filled from the station's tap and, 'bull at a gate', Johnny heaved his bulk up onto the boiler, squatting with his feet on the hand-rail. His mate handed him up the bucket of water just as the heat from the boiler got through to the skin of his knees. He gave an agonised yell, and half fell, half jumped backwards onto the platform, the bucket falling on top of his winded body while water, cascading over the boiler, went up in clouds of sizzling steam.

One of the smartest and probably better educated men on Westbourne Park shed from 1891 to 1900 was Charlie Hayes, a tubby, round-faced Herefordshire man. He had come to Slough as a fireman in 1864, aged nineteen, became a pilot driver in 1872 and thereafter distinguished himself on several occasions

for quick thinking in emergencies. In October 1885 he was a
2nd class driver with the o–6–o broad gauge engine *Tay*,
working long-haul goods trains as far as Wolverhampton and
Exeter, including the 10.25 p.m. Paddington to Plymouth,
known as 'The Tip'. He was driving the back working of this
train on 11 October 1885 and had passed Bath when a wagon
axle broke as the train was going around the gentle curves
through Sidney Gardens. Charlie was keeping a sharp look-out
to the rear as well as forwards, saw the wagon go down and
tumble across the down line, taking others with it, and stopped
quickly. He unhooked *Tay* and drove forward quickly to Bathampton where he was able to warn the signalman of the danger
and thus prevent a crash. Charlie Hayes stayed with broad
gauge engines until 29 May 1892, working with *Prometheus* until
October 1891 when he was given 3026 *Tornado*, one of Mr
Dean's brand new 'convertible' engines. William Dean,
Locomotive Superintendent of the Great Western, brought out
a powerful class of 7ft 8in. 'Singles' for the standard gauge but
equipped eight of them with broad gauge axles so that they
could take over the heavier broad gauge train from the old
Gooch 'eight-footers' which were frequently in great difficulty
owing to the weight of trains. When the gauge was changed
these eight were converted to the 4ft 8½in. gauge of the rest of
the class.

Fireman and driver took obligatory promotion as their turn
came, rising through eight grades from 3 shillings a day pilot
fireman at eighteen, to a 1st class engineman on 8 shillings a
day by the age of forty-three or thereabouts. Jim Street became
a pilot fireman in September 1895, at seventeen, working a
twelve-hour shift shunting or working empty coaches between
Paddington and west London sidings and sometimes firing on
the assisting engine to the train engine of long-haul freight
trains. Out shunting he was paired with eccentric, misfit or
simply worn-out drivers. In the first category there was one
man who solemnly informed him that blue-eyed people were
not to be trusted with a perambulator much less a locomotive

and so, as Jim had very blue eyes, he was the most undesirable of mates and would be treated accordingly. The misfits were 'put back' 1st class men who had done something dreadful and had been sentenced to a reduction in pay and a spell – or life – in the 'black gang' or the 'criminal link'. These links existed at several large centres where there was a great deal of boring 'trip' or shunting work to be done. The last category of men consisted of those whose health was suspect or failing or whose eyesight was not up to main line standards. Such men were 'put out to grass' either until their health improved or until they had worked their time and could retire at sixty or sixty-five with a pension from the Enginemen's and Firemen's Mutual Assurance Society.

Being pushed off into remote corners of the railway did nothing to improve the morale of men in the 'black gang' whilst the others were so close to retirement that discipline on the footplates of their shunting saddle tanks was slack. Many a night Jim drove and fired coal into the furnace over the prone and slumbering body of his mate curled up in front of the fire. Sometimes the driver was not even present but away on some secret and entirely predictable activity of his own. If his mate was not there Jim liked it better because then he could use the steam-brake to stop for each shunt which he could not do if he had his driver on the engine 'sleeping one off' since the explosive noise made when the steam-brake was released would disturb his slumbers. Shunting without the power-brake was tiring in the extreme, slamming the regulator shut on the shunter's 'stop' signal, whirling round and winding the hand-brake handle round furiously to bring the engine to a stand and then unwinding it. Luckily, Jim was strong and coped with these exhausting night-shifts. Young men of lesser physique might have been put off for life but for those who survived such difficulties only increased the value of the working experience they gained.

The best drivers cared for their engines as a coachman cared for his horse, developing a sensitivity to their needs and many drivers fussed over the machinery, bringing out the 'long feeder' oil can at every possible opportunity. The biggest engines of 1895 were of modest size – a 2–4–0 express engine was only 18 in. longer than the tender of a 'Castle' class engine – and faults were more readily noticeable on them than on the later, far larger, machines. If, on one of these nineteenth-century machines, an axle-box began to run hot, an alert driver would have his attention drawn to the fact by the jarring ride due to the heating box 'binding' in its guides and not moving up and down against its spring as the wheel travelled over the road. Feeling the rougher ride, the driver would watch each spring in turn to see which was 'dead' to know where the trouble lay. He would then attend to it straightaway, going along the footplating to oil it until the train could be stopped within the protection of fixed signals. Care for an engine sometimes turned into an obsession and a driver thus afflicted would watch his fireman's work jealously to ensure he was 'treating her right'. This would be agony for any fireman and could lead to harsh words and even fisticuffs. Passengers walking past an engine were sometimes alarmed to hear a violent argument or even to witness blows exchanged – it was known to happen – and the incident would lead to a fine for one or both men or even dismissal, all according to circumstances.

Keen engine drivers would 'shop around' to get the best fireman possible for the good of the engine and his coal bonus. A fireman, with a growing reputation for his skill and work-manlike manners, would remember all his life the day that some great driver recognised his worth and did him the honour of asking him to be his fireman. Jim once fired to the rising star of Westbourne Park's 'night goods' link, Ted Burden, which was a great honour for even then Ted was an 'ace' man and went on to great fame as Royal train driver. Ted was then, in 1896, a 2nd class, 7 shillings a day man and frequently worked express trains and on this occasion had to run a non-stop express from Paddington to Oxford with a 'Cobham' class 'Single' No 158. The engine was no larger than a big saddle-tank, about 25ft overall, but its big driving wheels made it capable of 60 mph with a skilled crew. Jim, who had only recently been made a 3rd class fireman, knew that the engine was due for a heavy repair and was 'shy for steam' and he asked Ted if he could put the 'hook' in the blast-pipe. The 'hook' was an old draw-bar coupling hook which, placed in the blast-pipe, constricted the orifice and thus increased the pressure of the exhaust blast; this then drew the fire more fiercely to generate more heat and thus coax steam from a reluctant boiler. Ted did not want to use it because it was against the rules and advertised its use by giving a distinctive sound to the exhaust note so the hook remained hidden under the coal at the back of the tender and off they went with their train.

They lost time all the way out to Reading and with no prospect of matters improving Ted decided that it was time for a little illegality and called for the hook to be brought. Jim went over the coal to fetch it and then kept watch from Ted's side of the cab while Ted went along the narrow footplating to the front of the engine with the heavy hook – and a chain to secure it – in one hand and held onto the boiler hand-rail with the other while the little engine nodded over the rail joints at 50 mph. The front platform was less than a foot wide. There he stood, stooped to lay down the ironmongery and undid the smokebox door handle which had been tightened on the shed by Jim with a good, firm, pull. Ted leant his weight forward on the polished handle, eased off the tension warily, spun it along its thread, withdrew the dart and swung the heavy steel door aside, risking being dragged off his narrow perch as the door, sail-like, was borne back against the slipstream. He then bent inside the smokebox, fixed the hook, pulled the door round against the slipstream and tightened the handle, leaning backwards to put all his weight on the thread while the engine bounced along at 50 mph. As a demonstration of cool-headedness – that most admirable of a driver's virtues – it took the laurels. The story went the rounds.

As a 3rd class fireman Jim's regular mate was Dave Daniels,

a good, conscientious driver who was a good mate and a willing teacher. They made a young, strong team who feared nothing and were willing to go anywhere – which was where 3rd class men were expected to go. They would work an 0–6–0 'Dean goods' down to Wolverhampton as assisting engine to the train engine of an overloaded Smithfield to Manchester meat train or down to Taunton with their own train of mixed freight, calling only at major stations. Sometimes they would arrive at Taunton with the fire run down low for shed and would be asked to take the train on to Exeter. The fire would be brought round and away they would go up the long bank to Whiteball tunnel and down into Devon – then the same thing would happen at Exeter and they would be asked to work on to Newton Abbot. They would have gone on to Plymouth just to set a new record for 'the cockneys'.

The majority of freight trains were hauled by large saddle-tanks and the heaviest coal trains were taken over the worst gradients by 0–6–0 engines with 4ft 6in. wheels, 17 in. x 24 in. cylinders driven by steam at 140 lb psi, and a water-tank capacity of only 1000 or 1100 gallons. Small engines, low speeds and limited water capacity combined to keep the enginemen on the road for long hours. When a fat old '1260' class saddle-tank on a long train of coal wagons came creeping to a stand at a wayside station's water column to replenish yet again its water-tank the signalman would go to his window and call out, 'If you want water, you'll have to go back inside – the fast's about.' Back into a refuge siding they would go and kick their heels for another hour until a favourable 'path' appeared for them on the main line. Enginemen were not allowed, by law, to work for more than 12 hours 'unless it is absolutely impossible to relieve them' and in the case of freight crews they were never relieved en route just because they had been on duty for 12 or 14 hours – they worked their train through to its destination however long it took. After 12 hours or so they would leave it 'dead' in a siding and go to shed with their engine, sleep where they could and then go back for their train and carry on. In foggy weather, particularly, the lot of a freight train crew was hard and uncertain as they never knew when they would finish work.

The 'diagrammed workings' of the engines and men were also eccentric in the 1890s. There was a job for a set of Swindon men with an 0–6–0 saddle-tank which set out from Swindon for South Wales as 'Pilot' engine assisting a heavily laden Hereford, Cheltenham and Swansea express up Sapperton bank and as far as Stroud. Here it was uncoupled and followed the express with a train of empty coal wagons for Gloucester, arriving about 7 p.m. The trucks were left in sidings and the engine worked round to the passenger station where it took the 9.15 p.m. fast train to Newport formed with two six-wheeled carriages and a freight brake van, calling only at Lydney and Chepstow. The carriages were left at Newport and, taking the brake van, the engine went up to Tydu (later Rogerstone) to pick up a train of Aberdare coal for Swindon. At 2 a.m. the real work of the night began as they set out for home hauling hundreds of tons of coal in loose-coupled, unbraked wagons over gradients and around curves on an all but invisible road. The guard in his brake van assisted his driver by applying and releasing his hand-brake as the gradients and signals required. All three men's knowledge of landmarks, their judgement of speed in the dark – the fireman had to know when to work the engine's hand-brake and how and when to fire coal – all their skill had to be uncanny or to appear so to outsiders, their alertness in the small hours of the morning had to be of a high order so that, night after night for years, 43½-ton engines could haul hundreds of tons of coal over a hilly ninety-mile route without a serious accident.

'Six coupled' goods engines of the tender variety were used on passenger trains as a matter of course. Jim Street and Dave Daniels would be 'diagrammed' to work a passenger train from Paddington to Maidenhead and back (tender first) with a 'Dean goods' before setting out on the real work of the night, a through freight to Wolverhampton. There were, at weekends, regular excursions to the riverside at Windsor and Henley in those days of straw boaters, striped blazers and ladies in long, white dresses – the Henley excursions were called 'Red Lion Expresses' by the enginemen. As the Foreman at Westbourne Park shed could not be sure when he would get his 2nd and 3rd class engine crews back off their journeys during Saturday he could not roster a specific set of men to an excursion so it was left to a kind of 'press-gang' arrangement where the men booking off late on Saturday afternoon or early evening would be detailed-off for an excursion in the morning. Some crews did all they could to get home early in order to be conscripted for some overtime, others would try to return late in the hope of missing the selection so they could have a Sunday off.

The most desirable special workings were the private charters, when an individual or small group who could afford the service would arrive on a station and order a train for his or her private use. This was a common enough practice in the 1890s and when the call came whichever set of enginemen were most quickly available would get the job – providing they knew the road. Jim Street and Dave Daniels were at Windsor one day when Lord Rothschild, fresh from an audience with Queen Victoria, came to the station and ordered a special to Aylesbury. One set of men turned the job down as they did not know the road but for the gold sovereign tip at the end of the run, Jim and Dave knew the road anywhere and took the job. They worked a special for Dame Nellie Melba once and for a group of Conservative politicians on another occasion. All these people had to do was ask, one engine and one carriage was all they required, the Great Western was only too happy to oblige and for a piece of gold so were Jim and Dave.

These 5-ft-wheeled 'Dean goods' engines managed relatively fast passenger work quite well, on freight all week, up and down on the 'Red Lion Expresses' on Saturday or Sunday or all the way to Malvern and back with an excursion. Only rarely did anything go wrong and when it did the enginemen paid the price. At midday on Monday 18 July 1898, Driver Wally Peart,

a long-serving, top link man and his 1st class fireman Henry
Dean were booked on 'spare' at Westbourne Park shed and
were ordered to prepare No 238, an o–6–o goods engine, for an
afternoon and evening on the Windsor run. Out with the 1.5
p.m. Paddington, all stations to the Royal borough, back with
the 4.15 p.m., stopping only at Slough and then two more
round trips before booking off at 9.30 p.m. Wally passed some
half-grumbling, half-joking remarks about the choice of engine
for this job to the Chief Locomotive Foreman, Alf Attwood,
who replied that the correct engine, 3240, a 6 ft 8½ in.-wheeled
2–4–o express engine had failed at Trowbridge so it was a
matter of make-do. Wally was not really concerned; 238 was
only nine months beyond a thorough repair and was in fine
condition. It had been on the Windsor run on Saturday and on
Sunday, he knew, Bob Philpin had had it on a heavy 'Red Lion'
and they had 'flown'.

In the shed yard, 238 was behind a 7-ft 'Single' which was
being prepared for a special to take the Cabinet down to
Windsor for an audience with the Queen. John Webb was in
charge, he and Wally exchanged the time of day, the two
engines were eventually coupled and they went together into
Paddington station for their respective trains. The special left
first, then Wally with the 1.5. At Windsor, Wally 'ran round'
his train, took 238 to turn on the triangular junction at Slough
and returned to Windsor where John Webb was still waiting
with the special in the yard for the return of the Cabinet from
Windsor Castle. Peart and Dean set out from Windsor at 4.15
with a heavy train of eleven eight-wheeled coaches and left
Slough on time at 4.24 with twenty-three minutes to cover 18¼
miles to Paddington. Brisk acceleration and a top speed of 60
mph was required to keep time.

Wally soon had the regulator wide open and, shortening the
valve travel a notch at a time, he had 238 snorting along at 55
mph by West Drayton. Henry Dean fired with the furnace
doors wide open; the boiler raised steam so well there was no
need to close them between shovels; the load was heavy; the fire

necessarily fierce and the heat from the open doors scorched Peart's trousers. Yet he only shifted his stance, kept his hand on the brake handle, his eyes on the road and let his engine tear into the load. Number 238 was a real little flyer. Its cylinders were within, between the frames and under the smokebox; the pistons driving on the central, cranked axle through connecting rods 6 ft long, 4 in. x 1½ in. thick. The rods lashed round, they whirled beneath the boiler, clearing the firebox front by inches where ¾ in. copper sheet held in steam at 160 lb psi, scalding water and at least half a ton of incandescent coal. Number 238 rocketed through Acton, past groups of passengers, its outside coupling rods skimming the platform edge, heading for Paddington at 60 mph.

The bang from the exploding boiler drowned all other sound, passengers spun round to face it and stood, transfixed, as the engine hurtled eastwards in a cloud of steam. Instantaneous with the volcanic bang the contents of the boiler and furnace erupted into the cab through the firehole. Henry Dean was blown off the footplate and killed. Wally Peart, to one side of the furnace, threw over the brake handle and then jumped off, horribly scalded from which injuries he subsequently died. The train came to a stand in 860 yds, the boiler and firegrate empty through a gaping rent in the firebox and tubeplate made where the stump of the broken, right-hand connecting rod had stabbed through. No one could have known that the rod was faulty; the 3-in. vertical flaw was internal and quite invisible.

TWO

Improvements by Accident

Wally Peart's last thought had been for his passengers when he braked his train before he jumped. The men were loyal to their public, the Company and to themselves through their pride in the job. They stuck to it through thick and thin, even to the death and the Company, in its paternalistic way, stood by them. The Chief Officers and lower supervisory grades were usually men who had spent years coming up from the ranks – though this was not always the case – so there was an understanding of the job at all levels and a mutual respect. Even the Directors valued their experienced 'servants'. There was, I feel, an air of decency at work on the Great Western though this could break down from time to time just as the men did not always maintain their high standards of public service and personal pride. The Great Western Railway was similar to an army, it was a *corps* of disciplined men bound together by a common purpose, by comradely feelings and often by adversity and hardship. It was, to use a modern expression, 'a good mob to be in'.

Richard Libby was a cleaner on Penzance shed in 1884, aged seventeen, and in 1887 became a pilot fireman on 'Buffalo' class saddle-tank No 1234. The engine was being driven slowly off the shed one day as Richard climbed onto the footsteps off the ground; he slipped and the front part of his right foot, up to the instep, was crushed under a driving wheel. The foot healed. He was fitted with a wooden limb by the GWR, returned to work and later was transferred to Plymouth as a 3rd class fireman. Part of his work now lay over the Princetown branch, 12 miles of single track winding up over the moor from Yelverton, on the Plymouth–Tavistock line, to the bleak little settlement around the prison. In some seasons it was a glorious job but in winter it was a kind of Siberia – complete with prison – and to set off from Yelverton onto that vast and desolate moor when it was deeply blanketed in snow – riding a semi-cabless engine – daily required a spirit of adventure.

On 19 February 1892 he was fireman on the 5.45 a.m. Plymouth to Princetown stone empties. Snow had been falling heavily and they worked bunker-first up the relatively sheltered, wooded, Plym valley so that when they reversed direction at Yelverton they would benefit from whatever protection the skimpy cab could give from the bitter weather over the moor. They arrived at Yelverton at 6.15 a.m., the signalman gave them the wooden Train Staff for the whole line through to the terminus – it was too early in the morning for Dousland, the only intermediate signal box on the line, to be open – and they set off into the wintery darkness without any knowledge of what lay ahead. The rails curved east, north and south, contouring and climbing at 1 in 40, the snow under the engine's wheels making the engine work harder, making Dick Libby use more coal. The driver was tense, waiting for the first wheel spin, ready to snap the regulator shut and ease it carefully open and all the time with no sight of what lay ahead. They trudged through Dousland station, dark and deserted, got round the horse-shoe curve above Meavy and Sheepstor villages where they might have stuck and set off north along the long straight. But the snow lay deeper as they climbed higher, the engine began to slip and they came to a shuddering, wheel-spinning halt by the crossing-keeper's house at Lowry.

They were stuck fast, 900 ft above sea-level, snow drifting in a menacing way around the driving wheels. Nothing less than another engine with a snow-plough would get them out but before any other train could enter the branch line the Train Staff had to be returned to Yelverton, $5\frac{1}{8}$ miles by serpentine railway, 2½ miles by snow-blocked road. The driver said he would have to stop with the engine so, after warming himself by the crossing-keeper's fire, Dick Libby set off limpingly to trek across the snowbound moor with the Train Staff. He got there safely, in spite of his lameness. The train was rescued and he was awarded 7s 6d by the Directors for his loyal service. It must have been a fairly regular occurrence – getting snowed-in – but rewards from Directors could not have followed every feat of walking – that would have been expecting too much!

On 28 January 1898 Bill Hatherall, a twenty-one-year-old fireman was working the 5.45 a.m. Plymouth when it got stuck in a cutting 800 yds short of Princetown station. Bill stayed with the engine while his mate went into the station to get help. Hours later a fresh fireman came out to stand guard over the locomotive and next day, when the snow eased off, Hatherall set off to walk this lonely seven-mile road in the wake of a blizzard, to carry the Train Staff back to Yelverton. Perhaps it was because he was not a cripple, perhaps the Directors could not afford to fork out 7s 6d for each occasion a fireman accomplished this arduous task but all they could muster for Bill Hatherall was a 'Commendation'.

South-east of Princetown, in the lush green valley of the river Dart, lay Ashburton, an ancient town which had recently become the terminus for a 9½ miles long, single-track, broad-gauge branch line off the main line near Totnes. Just before the change of gauge in May 1892 the railway was signalled by the (wooden) Train Staff and (card) Ticket system with electric 'block instruments' by which the men could exchange routine signalling messages between the 'block sections': Ashburton Junction signal box (on the main fast line) to Staverton; Staverton to Buckfastleigh; Buckfastleigh to Ashburton. At each of the three stations the semaphore signals were worked by a signal-porter using a frame of levers on the platform, the electric instruments were in the Station Inspector's office and operated by him while each point – to switch a train to the 'passing loop' or into the goods yard – was moved by a lever on the track or the sleeper end close to the blade of the point it worked. To prevent the points being set one way and the signals being pulled for another a system of return wires and slotted, metal plates gave some sort of interlocking protection.

On 12 May 1892 the Station Inspector for the pretty station at Buckfastleigh was away on railwaymen's 'Provident Society' business and the next senior man, Edwin Bartlett, had been left in charge. He had worked the station for years and that morning had booked on at 6.45 for a thirteen-hour shift with an hour break. Besides him on the station was Bill Bond, a long-serving signal-porter and the 'strapper', George Lang, with only four years' service. The station did a healthy trade and by lunchtime three wagons of merchandise were loaded, ready for the pick-up goods to carry them away to the main line. But this train, the 10.20 a.m. from Newton Abbot to Ashburton and back, was running four hours late and left Totnes at 4.15 p.m. behind an 0-6-0 engine, driven by Bob Miller, with George Peters as guard. The fireman's name is not known. They were all on a twelve-hour shift which now looked like turning into a sixteen-hour day even if nothing else delayed them and they may well have been considering staying the night in Totnes once they had brought the valley traffic out onto the main line.

The train reversed into the yard at Staverton to pick up traffic from the flour mill and leave off empties. While they were shunting, a down passenger train called at the station and left at 3.50, leaving the Staff for the goods and carrying a Ticket as authority to occupy the single track to Buckfastleigh. Bob Miller pulled out of the little yard with nineteen wagons and two brake vans at 4.20 and left carrying the Staff down to Buckfastleigh because the next train requiring to travel over that section would be coming from that station.

Edwin Bartlett was getting very concerned about the paper and wool – from his staple customers – which ought to have been on its way to London and had not even started towards Ashburton – so when he knew that the goods was actually on its way from Staverton he decided on his plan. The goods engine would put the three wagons on the passing loop and the 4.40 Ashburton–Totnes passenger train could take them. The goods arrived on the platform line at 4.30, the engine was hurriedly uncoupled 'behind the Buckfasts' which it then drew forwards, under the road bridge towards Ashburton prior to pushing them back into the little yard. Station staff and train crew worked fast – they all knew that the 4.40 Ashburton would soon be 'about'. The 'Buckfast' traffic was dropped, the three 'Londons' were hooked on, drawn out to the bridge, points switched and the wagons reversed into the passing loop. The engine then rejoined its train in the platform at 4.38. At that moment Ashburton asked 'Is Line Clear?' on the block instrument for the passenger train. In two seconds the realisation passed through Bartlett's mind that he would have to shunt the goods onto the passing loop and, because of the three wagons to go up to Totnes, the goods would have to reverse in from the Ashburton end which would require the train to draw onto the single track to clear the loop points. The entire 'forward and back' shunt would take seven minutes so if he obeyed the rules and 'refused the road' until the line was clear he would delay the passenger at Ashburton by five minutes; if he gave 'Line Clear' the train would not arrive for seven minutes – just long enough to get the goods train out of the way. He pegged his instrument to 'Line Clear' and told George Lang, who was in the office, to run and tell Bill Bond to hurry with the shunt. George ran onto the platform with the message and George Peters, the guard protested. 'That won't do – you can't go outside if you've given "Clear" for the passenger.' 'We can if we're quick,' said the signal-porter, 'the 4.40 won't be here for minutes yet.' Bob Mitchell, nothing loth, drove his train out onto the single line.

The 4.40 from Ashburton was formed with two 3rd class carriages and a composite 1st/3rd/brake-van, hauled by a 2–4–0 saddle-tank called *Bury* with Driver Norton (twenty years' service), Fireman Palmer (five years' service) and John Smerdon, an old South Devon Railway guard (thirty-three years' service). Norton saw Buckfastleigh's distant signal at

'Caution' half a mile before he passed it, took less than cautious note of it and let the train rattle on at 30 mph. His preview of the stop signal against the Ashburton side of the road bridge was practically nil due to the curvature of the line and overhanging trees. He came sailing happily down the grade on a lovely sunny May afternoon, rounded the bend and was confronted simultaneously by a signal at 'Danger' and broad front of the goods engine barely 200 yds away. He braked hard, he and his mate got down on the footsteps of the cab and jumped just before the 15 mph collision. The travelling public got a rare old shaking though, as usual, the stability of the broad gauge was a factor in their favour – and all this the consequence of Edwin Bartlett's strong desire to please all of his customers all of the time.

The conversion of the gauge during 21/22 May 1892 – after two weeks' preparation – from Brunel's carefully conceived 7 ft 0¼ in. to Stephenson's ill-considered 4 ft 8½ in. was probably the longest delayed event in the history of railways and marked the start of what E.T. McDermott, the Company's official historian, called 'The Great Awakening'. There was plenty to do if the Brunellian dash of 1844–52 was to be restored. E. Foxwell, in his book *Express Trains: English and Foreign*, described the Great Western of 1889 very well when he wrote: 'The Great Western is a very solid line and makes its progress in a stolid style, doing some great things and many small but all alike with the immovability of Jove.' The one great achievement of Great Western management and men in the otherwise technically undistinguished years from 1852 until 1892 when express trains were de-cellerated (and for a time, from 1864, abolished) was the building of the Severn tunnel, 7668 yds long, opened in January 1886. It was not until 1888 that the swivelling bogie was placed beneath Great Western carriages as a matter of course and not until 1892 that the Company made it their normal practice to construct gas-lit, steam-heated, corridor-connected coaches running on two four-wheel bogies. And it took years to replace all old carriages with modern stock, for example, the rape-oil roof-lamps immortalised in Thomas Hardy's poem 'Midnight on the Great Western' and the metal hot-water bottles took twenty-three years and twelve years respectively to be phased out of service.

The improvements owed nothing to the gauge change which was no more than a conveniently dramatic marker for long overdue reform and everything to the pressures of competition and the passing-on of the old men in charge of the line. Sir Daniel Gooch, Chairman of the Board since 1865, had died in harness in October 1889 and George Nugent Tyrrell, who had been appointed Superintendent of the Line in 1864 because of his love of economy and dislike of express trains, had retired in June 1888. His assistant, N.J. Burlinson, took over and began a very cautious policy of increasing the speed and the numbers of fast trains and of admitting 3rd class passengers to their hallowed compartments. All this was twenty years and more behind the other two great Companies – the 'North Western Railway and the Midland Railway – and was all 'on paper' until locomotives more powerful than the old Gooch 'Singles' could be built to turn the West of England timetables' promises into fact.

The most beautiful locomotives ever to run on rails were, in the opinion of all right-thinking people, William Dean's '3001' class of 7 ft 8 in. 'Single wheelers' but they were, on reflection, the ugly ducklings of the steam engine world. The prototype, 3021 *Wigmore Castle*, came out of Swindon works in April 1891 as a 'convertible', its great, spoked driving wheels standing out crudely naked beyond the standard gauge frames. The standard gauge machines, starting with 3001 *Amazon*, were slightly less ungainly, having their wheels hidden decently behind the frames but they were all squat, 'dumpy'-looking engines as one might expect from a machine which carried its 44 tons on only three axles and their subsequent transformation into the uttermost peak of Victorian locomotive elegance was the direct result of this original sin.

Charlie Hayes had driven 3021 since it was converted to the

standard gauge and on 16 September 1893 was booked on at 7.55 a.m. for a 5 p.m. finish, to work the 'crack' nine o'clock express from Paddington to Exeter and another one home. His usual mate was suddenly not available and at short notice John Webb had given him a 3rd class fireman for the job, Bill Gibbons. They took the engine slowly along the siding to Green Lane signal box with four young cleaners clinging to it like grimy bees, giving copper and brass a final rub. They got off when the engine stopped at the signal guarding the exit to the main line and in due course 3021, glittering with gorgeous colours, rolled smoothly back into Paddington station. The train's Head Guard, Bill Nalder – thirty-two years in the service – was waiting by the coaches in his frock coat with a seasonal flower in the lapel while Junior Guard John Hutchings, sixteen years on the railway, attended to the stowing of luggage in the front van where he rode as 'Front Guard'; Bill Nalder was 'Rear Guard'. Bill greeted Charlie Hayes affably – they had worked together for many years – and gave him the load, 'Ten eights and a six-wheel slip-coach for Didcot,' about 250 tons in all – a very heavy load for 3021 especially as the fireman was relatively inexperienced. There were few fast trains to the West and this, the first of the day, was formed to the maximum capacity of the engine. They left at 9 a.m. and immediately began to lose time as Charlie had to coax the 'Single' gently into speed because the single pair of driving wheels were liable to skid if handled roughly with such a load. More time was lost when Bill Gibbons allowed the boiler to become too full of water so that some was carried over into the cylinders. The train was delayed outside Reading station's antiquated, 1840s layout and though *Wigmore Castle* made a brave sight as it steamed brassily through the green of the Thames valley it was losing time and the slip-coach was dropped at Didcot twenty minutes behind time. Gradients were rather steeper through the Vale of the White Horse but young Bill had the job well in hand by then and Charlie was able to hold to the schedule until they were brought to a stand at Ashbury Crossing. Dragging through Shrivenham, half a mile further on they saw the cause of the delay: the station was crowded with soldiers and their train was backed onto the up line to allow them to pass. They were twenty-five minutes late into Swindon. Charlie Hayes knew what to expect and sure enough, as he brought the train gently alongside the platform for the compulsory ten-minute stop, there was the familiar figure, bowler hatted and hands on hips, of Inspector William Greenaway.

Bill Greenaway had started as a labourer in Swindon factory aged seventeen in 1860 and was an 'eight bob a day man' at Bristol driving the broad gauge 'Single' *Timour* at the time of his promotion to Inspector in 1889*. He knew Charlie well and understood why many of the Company's best trains ran late for he had often had to coax *Timour* along with an overloaded express. There were either too few engines to run enough trains to meet demand or much more powerful engines were needed. William Dean knew this but the Directors did not. They commanded that 'something had to be done' – provided that it did not cost anything. Bill Greenaway was that 'something'; he rode on the footplates of late-running trains and tried not to get in the fireman's way.

During the ten-minute obligatory stop for the consumption of Swindon refreshment room's notorious pork pies, Charlie Hayes re-filled the locomotive's lubricator with oil and the train 'set sail'. Westward through the signal boxes the signal-men belled out 'Is Line Clear for an express train?' until the '4 beats' code rang out from Corsham West to Box Tunnel East End box where George Bowden pegged 'Line Clear' in reply and pulled his down home and distant signals at 11.44 – twenty-eight minutes late. He expected to see the engine working hard, making up time, but it approached very sedately and trundled into the tunnel at 45 mph as Box Station No 1 box asked the road for the 11.3 Bristol to Swindon stopping train at

---

* Photograph of Bill Greenaway in Plate 15 of *Grub, Water & Relief: Tales of the Great Western 1835–1892*, John Murray, 1985.

11.50. 3021 had been priming after Chippenham, Charlie had shut off steam and the engine went into the tunnel free-wheeling with steam roaring deafeningly from the safety-valves. The track was brand new, cross-sleepered, relaid three weeks before so the enginemen stood disoriented in the cacophonous dark, unable to see or hear movement and barely able to feel any. For ninety seconds they stood patiently waiting to clear the tunnel, to escape the awful, blinding din when the engine suddenly 'hunted' viciously left and right at the leading end. Charlie Hayes grabbed for the brake, missed and fell; the others instinctively grabbed hold of solid objects; the 'hunting' continued; the spring-hanger rod on the left-hand leading wheel broke at a welding flaw; the track spread out of gauge; the engine mounted the inner rail and ran straddling it. Charlie, back on his feet, braked hard, the engine slewed round, over-turned its tender and came to a stand upright, with the leading wheels in the up line track. It was 11.52, the up stopping train was passing Box No 1 and its 'Entering Section' bell tolled out in George Bowden's cabin.

Hayes' and Greenaway's first thoughts were for the up train. They had no detonators to put down; they were lost in the buried, buckled tool box on the upturned tender; they had no light to wave because the shaking had extinguished the gauge lamp. Greenaway and Gibbons began frantically to search for some paper to take a light off the engine's fire for the lamp's wick while Charlie Hayes blew the brake whistle. The noise of 3021's safety-valve competed with the deep, booming whistle so he gave up, got off the engine and groped his way along the tunnel wall towards Box. The tunnel was full of smoke so that the entrance, quarter of a mile away, was invisible. There would be no chance of a little oil lamp being seen even if they had one. Then, he heard the sound of the stopping train's engine, steaming hard, and, as it drew nearer, so did the passengers on the 9 a.m. Paddington. All ten coaches were de-railed but upright and those that were not trapped by their legs in wreckage got down on the floor, some to pray, as the noise of the up train's urgent exhaust swelled through the roaring of 3021's escaping steam.

The 11.3 Bristol was hauled by a 2–4–0 express engine No 3240, driven by Tom Kelling and fired by Fred Hales. Charlie Hayes had managed to get a hundred yards or so from the wreck when the engine passed him invisible save for its head-lamp, sparks from an unseen chimney and firelight on flying smoke. '*Stop!*' he yelled. Kelling was startled, turned his head and turned back again before braking – just as his engine crashed into 3021 and ripped past. The two trains interlocked, the up train getting the worst of it, 3240 smashing her cylinders, her outside coupling rods were sliced off, her dome and cab crushed. Tom Kelling was thrown against the boiler and broke his shoulder. Fred Hales was knocked unconscious and buried under a torrent of coal from the tender. Kelling's watch was crushed with the hands at 11.54 a.m.

The cause of the crash was a broken front axle on 3021 which served to focus attention on the heavy strain placed on the leading axle of the Great Western's principal express engines and as a result they were all fitted with a four-wheel bogie under the front end, thus achieving – literally 'by accident' – the most handsome engine in the world and probably the most successful 'Single Wheeler'.

On 12 November 1895 an event took place of the greatest significance to the Company since the opening of the Severn tunnel: Swindon station's refreshment room lessee was bought out. For £100,000 the Great Western rid itself of the compul-sory ten-minute stop which had lain like a toll-bar across the route since 1841 and which would otherwise have remained until 1940. The lease was formally surrendered on that day but its enormous significance was first seen on 1 October when the down 'Cornishman' ran through Swindon to make the first non-stop run in excess of 100 miles in the history of the Great Western by covering 118½ miles, Paddington to Bristol, in 135 minutes. The consequences went much deeper; long, non-stop runs required other means of feeding the passengers and, thirty years after their introduction on the 'North Western Railway and Midland Railway, the restaurant car appeared, in May 1896, on some Great Western expresses for the use of 1st class passengers only. In July that year the first non-stop runs between Paddington and Exeter were instituted, 194 miles in 3¾ hours, the longest, fastest, non-stop train service in the world. To enable such feats water-troughs were laid between the rails at Basildon, near Goring, and at Fox's Wood, near Bristol, so that engines' tenders could be re-filled at speed by the lowering of a scoop below each tender. None of this would have been of any use without an improved lubrication system for the slide valves and pistons of the engines. When all expresses called at Swindon and the longest non-stop run was 77 miles, it sufficed to have a lubricator holding a pint of oil up front on the smokebox side which the driver adjusted with great delicacy to deliver just enough oil to last the journey; drivers would refill the vessel during the Swindon stop. Now, however, a larger lubricator was called for and one was provided in the engine's cab, fitted with a glass tube through which the oil passed in drops enabling the driver to see – for the first time – the rate of flow and adjust it with more certainty.

William Dean's 'Singles' worked the new expresses to Exeter and his handsome, 6 ft 8 in. driving wheel 2–4–0 engines handled the South Wales expresses. They were good machines, better than most, but still none too powerful for the job in hand. In October 1899, Dean's principal assistant, G.J. Churchward, brought out from Swindon works his prototype boiler, a very much more effective steam-raiser than any which had gone before and destined to be developed, year by year, until its principles were incorporated in the British Railways 'Standard' designs of 1951. This boiler, mounted on a 4–4–0 engine with 5 ft 8 in. driving wheels, was named – rather unfortunately – *Camel* which became the 'class' name until the more evocative name 'Bulldog' became attached to the class. The 'Camel' or 'Bulldog' class was the root, the first, careful step towards a whole range of very powerful engines. All that was lacking at the turn of the century from the Great Western's modernisation programme was a truly effective brake. The Company were unaware of any shortcomings in this direction; it took an accident to show them up and thereby hangs a tale.

Just before dawn on 16 June 1900, Driver Henry Woodman, who had begun his career in the Bristol & Exeter Railway sheds at Bristol, breakfasted, put a large steak-and-kidney pie his wife had made into his big, black metal box along with the spare gauge glasses and woollen 'trimmings', rule-books and time-tables, closed the domed lid and set off for Bristol, Bath Road, shed. He met his fireman, young Henry Cann at the gate – Cann was a 1st class fireman after only seven years' service – and together they walked to the time office to book-on at 5.30 a.m. Together they prepared their engine, Dean 'Single' 3015 *Kennet* for the road, checking everything, building a fire, oiling round, then took it to the station and hooked onto the rapidly filling coaches of the 6.30 a.m. stopping train to Paddington. They arrived safely at 10.30 a.m., took *Kennet* to Westbourne Park shed and left it in the care of a shed turner before walking round to the Mint coffee tavern, Henry Cann carrying his driver's box and walking a pace or two behind, as befited a young and respectful fireman in the presence of so majestic an old-hand driver. Woodman took this for granted but was not aloof, indeed, he donated a large slice of the rich steak-and-kidney pie to his young mate to enliven his dull bread and cheese.

Food and non-alcoholic drink consumed, they strolled back to the shed, looked round their engine and at 12.50 took it along the engine line to Green Lane signal box, coming to a stand behind the engine for the 1.5 p.m. express to Windsor. Henry Cann went across to the box to give the 'bobby' the tip – '3015 for the 1.15 Falmouth' – and rejoined Woodman on the engine. They were let out at 1 p.m. and *Kennet* rolled imperturbably back onto its train. They watched the 1.5 leave, snaking across the points from Platform 4 to the down main, and dead on time at 1.15 they got their own 'Right Away', straight down the main from Platform 1. Cann began firing coal at Royal Oak and the elegant engine accelerated its heavy train, riding with the unique smoothness of a 'Single Wheeler'.

On the down main line at Slough the 1.5 Paddington was delayed by the large amounts of passengers' luggage and parcels to be unloaded. The tail of the train was level with Slough East box at the London end of the platform. The signalman had given 'Train out of Section', as he was entitled to do, back to Dolphin Junction, the next box east, towards London and when the signalman at Dolphin 'asked the road' for the 1.15 Paddington, the Slough East man replied with the 'Warning Acceptance', 3–5–5 beats on the bell indicating that while the section between the two boxes was clear Slough station was blocked within 440 yds of the protecting home signal. As a result of receiving this bell code the Dolphin Junction man kept his signals at 'Danger' and waited for the express to come to a stand at his home signal which he would then lower – or 'take off', to use the still-surviving broad gauge parlance – and, as the train approached him at very reduced speed, he would hold a red flag from his window. When the engine had stopped opposite his box he would shout across to the driver that the section ahead was clear but the line ahead of Slough East's home signal was occupied. A green flag would then authorise the driver to proceed.

Henry Woodman had *Kennet* flying. Henry Cann was firing smoothly, boiler pressure was 'on the mark', everything was as sound as a bell. Perhaps Woodman had eaten too much steak-and-kidney pie and it was lying heavily in his stomach; at any rate he was well content and did not see the red arm of Dolphin's distant signal standing at 'Danger'. The signalman at Dolphin was puzzled when he heard no protesting whistle from this, one of the 'crack' trains of the day, passing signals which intended to arrest its 60 mph flight and became down-right alarmed when 3015 shot under the near-by bridge, steaming hard. He ran to his bell, sent 4–5–5 'Train Running Away' to Slough East and ran back to his window to wave a red flag. Henry Woodman saw nothing. Henry Cann looked up from his firing to watch the signals and was horrified to see, through the arch of a bridge ahead, Slough East's home signal at 'Danger' and the rear of the 1.5 Paddington just beyond it. The regulator handle was pushed right over towards him, it took a single thrust of his arm to slam it shut and, still moving, to throw the handle of the combined steam and vacuum brake to 'brakes on'. Only then did Woodman realise what was happening, instantly reversing the engine and applying sand under the wheels through the steam-powered jet. They had 700 yds in which to stop, the gap closing with terrifying rapidity. Henry Woodman hauled down on both whistle chains as his fireman wrenched the tender hand-brake on as tight as he could. Down at the station, warned by Slough East signalman's yells, staff were moving people out of the rear of the train and trying to get it moving.

The brakes of 3015 were operated by steam cylinders fitted with pistons which were driven out by steam and, through rodding, pressed brake blocks against the wheels. The carriage wheels were braked by a vacuum system. There was slightly less than one minute for the brakes to bring the train to a stand but steam condenses impotently to water on cold cast-iron and *Kennet*'s steam-brake cylinders were stone cold. The train's brake took time to work because air, at atmospheric pressure to drive the pistons in their vacuum chambers, had to travel the entire length of the train from the driver's admission valve. For a certain distance there was no brake at all on the engine while the carriage brakes came on slowly, axle by axle. The 1.5 Paddington had just started to move when the 1.15 crashed into its rear at 25 mph.

The Great Western had been very proud of its brakes and its safety record and was caused considerable embarrassment by the crash. However, because every weakness in their system had been shown up, including the length of time it took to release the brakes on the 1.5, a truly effective brake was devised. This included, among other things, a very powerful 'ejector' to expel air from the vacuum system; a vacuum brake on most engines; and on each carriage brake cylinder a 'direct admission' valve which opened in proportion to the driver's application of the brake to allow air directly into the cylinders and thus make a quicker application than if air had to pass all through the length of the train pipe. The Great Western braking system soon surpassed all other vacuum brakes in power and smoothness of application and remained in use for seventy years.

THREE

Breaking Records

In March 1902 the Great Western was asked to provide a Royal train to take King Edward and Queen Alexandra to Kingswear and Plymouth. The King was to lay the foundation stone of Britannia Royal Naval College at Dartmouth and the Queen was to launch the battleship HMS *Queen* from Devonport. Just two years before, in April 1900, Churchward had out-shopped from Swindon works his first express locomotive, to all practical purposes a 'Camel' class with 6 ft 8½ in. driving wheels, to be known as an 'Atbara' class. They were fast and, with the new-type 'Camel' boiler, powerful engines for the times. The Great Western used them on their new, 'crack' Exeter expresses. Acutely conscious of the value of publicity (the precise opposite to Paddington's attitude ten years previously) the Great Western was anxious not to hide its light under a sleeper – and what better advertisement in those intensely loyal times than a Royal train? The Great Western Directors decided to run the train non-stop – 229 miles to Kingswear in 4 hours 27 minutes, far away the longest non-stop run in the kingdom – and ordered that the water troughs being installed at Creech, near Taunton, be finished immediately to enable the run to take place. Sir Joseph Wilkinson, the Great Western's General Manager, was sent round to Marlborough House to hand in the plans to the King's secretary, Sir Frank Knollys; the King himself studied and approved them; and on 7 March 1902 at 10.30 a.m. the record-breaking Royal train set out from Paddington.

The engine was 3374 *Baden Powell*, renamed *Britannia*, and

the train consisted of an eight-wheel van next to the engine; a
1st class carriage for the First Lord of the Admiralty, Earl
Selborne and Admirals Fawkes and Fullerton; a Double saloon
for two ladies and two gentlemen attendants for the King and
Queen; the Royal saloon carrying the King, Queen and Princess Victoria; and the Directors' saloon, somewhat crowded
with the Chairman, Lord Cawdor, Deputy Chairman, Mr
Robinson, Colonel Edgecumbe, G.C. Mott and Ernest Palmer,
Directors, plus the principal Officers of the Company. Their
saloon had a wide observation window in the trailing end and,
as a lure to get His Majesty to visit them, the Directors
'provided a gangway between the Royal saloon and their own
so that the King could make use of the latter for a more
comprehensive view of the country'.

If the King used the Directors' saloon he would have seen the
silhouette of a policeman on every over-bridge and at least one
plate-layer guarding every footpath or farmtrack across the
line. There were no delays, the train arrived in Kingswear two
minutes early at 2.55 p.m. and the Royal party walked down to
the GWR pontoon where the ferry *Dolphin*, dressed overall, was
waiting. Needless to say, every plank and post of the jetty was
swathed in bunting and the narrow streets were thronged with
cheering townspeople. On the bridge of the heavily be-flagged
Dolphin, a gold-braid-entwined Captain Beatty, RN, gave the
signal to start and the little ferry boat swung away across the
Dart for Dartmouth. King Edward did his bit with the foundation stone briskly, they were all back in the train by 4 p.m. and
at 5. 25 arrived in cheering Devonport. Here the Royal party
transferred to the Royal yacht by way of the Great Western's
tender, the PS *Sir Richard Grenville*, temporarily under the
command of a naval officer. Next day Queen Alexandra laun-
ched her battleship and retired to the yacht *Victoria and Albert*
until Monday morning, her wedding anniversary.

The Royal couple came ashore from *Sir Richard Grenville* at
Prince's pier, Millbay dock, where their train was waiting. The
five magnificent vehicles stood with slack couplings in order to

negotiate the sharply curved tracks set in the cobbled quay and was headed by a pair of 0–6–0 saddle-tanks, ex-Cornwall Mineral Railways, placed back to back or bunker to bunker. These two diminutive engines hauled the train to Millbay Junction without a jolt where, in precisely the five minutes alloted, the tanks were removed, the couplings screwed taut and *Britannia* placed proudly at the head of the train. To mark the anniversary a board carrying the Arms of Great Britain and Denmark was fitted to the front of the glittering engine which set off, dead on time, at 11.40 a.m. From Millbay to Paddington the route was lined on both sides by cheering, handkerchief-waving people and between the show of national pride, loyalty and affection 3374 drew the King and Queen at 60 miles an hour. The journey was completed 1½ minutes early at an overall average of 52 mph, 246½ miles in 4 hours 48 minutes. His Majesty was delighted and personally congratulated Sir Joseph Wilkinson. The one detail overlooked in official reports was the name of the first Great Western fireman ever to work through from Plymouth to Paddington on a non-stop express.

The following year the Prince and Princess of Wales made a tour of the West Country starting from Plymouth. Prince George asked for a special effort to be made so on 14 July the five-coach Royal train set off from Paddington behind Church-ward's latest locomotive development, a 'Super Atbara', an 'Atbara' with a bigger, more cunningly contrived boiler which went under the name of the 'City' class, 3433 *City of Bath*. The driver was the steel-nerved Ted Burden – fireman unrecorded as usual – but he did the Royal couple proud: the train passed Chippenham at 80 mph and covered the 117 miles to the Bristol Avoiding Line Junction in 102 minutes. The unnamed fireman shovelled coal as no fireman had ever done before on the Great Western so that, in spite of the slowings on the single-track sections along the Dawlish sea wall and the final thirty miles of line containing the steepest gradients and sharpest curves of any main line in Britain, the train averaged 63½ mph from start to stop and covered the 246½ miles in 3¾ hours.

The Great Western had run the 'Cape Mail' boat-express to Plymouth in broad gauge days but it took the glamour of the huge, transatlantic liners, which were racing each other across 3000 miles of stormy water, to set the men of the Great Western and London & South Western into a fever of competitiveness. In 1903 North German Lloyd and Hamburg–Amerika lines began to disembark at Plymouth passengers from their New York to Southampton liners. The London & South Western Railway took the passengers while the Great Western took the mail and the gold bullion which was a feature of transatlantic cargoes at that time. The 'Ocean Liner' specials were instantly 'sacred' to the men, who instigated a race. The Companies could not order them to do so and from the moment the great ship dropped anchor outside the Breakwater the race was on. Outright competition was abandoned after the horrible crash of a L & SWR boat-train at Salisbury on 1 July 1906 but the 'Ocean Liner' specials remained, on the GWR and later British Railways, as the 'crack' trains of the West of England route for fifty years and are now part of its legend.

A few of the gallant men whose daring created that legend are recorded – Drivers Millard, Uren and Clements, all from Exeter shed, and one of the Inspectors who rode with them, G.H. Flewellyn. Typically, no one bothered to record the names of the most important men of all – the firemen. G.H. Flewellyn began as a cleaner on Bristol shed in April 1878, aged sixteen; he became a pilot fireman after six years; and passed as a driver in January 1893. Promotion to driver came in April 1897 at Plymouth and from the position of 3rd class driver he was promoted to Inspector at Newton Abbot in June 1901. He was a handsome, 'well-set-up' man in his prime, who seemed to become stooped or rather shrunken in later life, a man of neat, precise and careful habits yet bold enough for all that. Only once in his long career was he reprimanded and that was for erring on the side of caution. While he was a fireman he refused to work a train over Whiteball bank from Taunton because he believed the engine to be overloaded. He eventually had to take the train up without an assisting engine and the climb was achieved without trouble but the argument at Taunton had caused delay so he was given a mild rebuke. After he became Chief Inspector at Swindon he gained Great Western-wide respect for his knowledge and his fair dealing with drivers and firemen.

The London & South Western took the Ocean traffic so seriously that they had their Chief Locomotive Superintendent, Dugald Drummond, riding on the engines of the special trains – which must have been a nerve-racking experience for the poor enginemen, given Drummond's fearsome reputation for discipline. On 23 April 1904 the London & South Western broke all records by getting a boat-train from Plymouth to Waterloo in 4 hours 3 minutes. Great Western drivers were bursting to be 'up and at 'em', bursting to unleash their 'City' class engines which were undoubtedly better machines than the London & South Western's 4–4–0s but Great Western track was still in process of being upgraded to cope with modern power and Churchward told Flewellyn to restrain his men saying, in true Churchwardian style, 'Withhold any attempt at a record till I give the word – then you can go and break your bloody necks.'

He gave the word early in May and on the 9th, 3440 *City of Truro* pulled away from Plymouth Millbay dock with five vans of mail and bullion off the SS *Kronprinz* which had dropped anchor eighty-seven minutes earlier. The enthusiasm of the GWR Marine Department was shared by Driver Moses Clements, his unnamed fireman* and Inspector Flewellyn on 3440. Clements set *City of Truro* to storm Dartmoor and his mate bent his back most loyally, enabling the 148-ton train to career across the southern slopes of the moor at astonishing speeds, uphill and down dale, around the constant succession

---

* It has been claimed by a descendant of the man, in a letter to me, that one William Brecknell was the fireman. My research has shown that a man of that name became a Pilot driver at Exeter in January 1904. It is possible that, with a record run in mind, Flewellyn wanted a highly skilled fireman for the job and booked to the special a man of Brecknell's seniority.

of sharp curves, thundering over tall viaducts. They cleared
Dainton summit at almost 60 mph after two miles climbing at
an average of 1 in 80 and after twenty miles of stiff climbing
tipped over the Whiteball summit at 53 mph. How that fireman
must have worked! Bent double, swing from the waist, forward
and back from tender to firehole, plying his shovel with precise,
practised, aimed strokes as the engine rocketed around the
curves with Flewellyn and Clements clinging on tight to the cab
hand-rails.

Whoever the fireman was he must have been entirely thankful when the engine climbed the ridge out of Devon and shot
downhill through the tunnel into Somerset; he could take a
breather, or so he thought. But Clements let 3440 fly. Have you
ever seen the curves down that side of Whiteball bank? Our
hero must have been sitting with his hair standing on end as
sharp bends raced towards the engine, seeming sharper than
ever before as speed rose to insane levels, yet the careful
Flewellyn never said 'Whoa', and the engine was steaming like
a runaway. Then, as they rounded a curve and were thundering
down a short straight a group of saviours appeared in the form
of the local permanent-way gang and Moses, not wanting to
end up beneath a fiery chariot, took this opportunity to put the
brakes on hard and bring the speed down to a sensible 65 mph.
Someone had to call it quits and this way he could do it without
appearing to have lost his nerve. Back in the train itself a
certain 'railwayac' called Charles Rous-Marten forgot he was a
gentleman and swore. He was timing the train and his stop-
watch had just recorded a quarter-mile run at 97.8 mph; the
next quarter-mile appeared to have been run at 102.3 mph and,
just as he was timing another for confirmation, the brakes went
on. Damn it! Speed soon rose and 3440 continued its 75 mph
gallop across Somerset by the virtue of that unknown fireman
shovelling coal as steadily as if his arms were part of the
machinery – which, in a sense, they were. At Pylle Hill, Bristol,
City of Truro and one van was detached and Dean 'Single' *Duke
of Connaught* backed on. The 7 ft 8 in. driving wheels, three parts

hidden behind the frames, turning without visible means, gave the impression that the engine was gliding over the rails and thus, deceptively, took the train to Paddington, 118¾ miles in ninety-nine minutes in spite of a dead slow crawl at Swindon so that the gold from the SS *Kronprinz* landed at Paddington in 3¾ hours from Plymouth, just over five hours after the ship dropped anchor outside The Sound.

This tale has been told before but I can hardly ignore it. Less well known are the magnificent developments which the Great Western carried out at Fishguard. Here, remote on the Pembrokeshire coast, a new harbour was carved out of the sheer cliff, new railways were constructed to connect it to the existing network and also, far inland, to shorten the route to Wales. The dock opened for traffic – though not then completed – on 30 August 1906. At first it was used by boats and trains on the Irish run, the 8.45 a.m. and 8.45 p.m. 'Cork Expresses' becoming at least as heavy and important as the recently established 'Cornish Riviera'. New trains were constructed for the Irish traffic and 1st and 3rd class passengers could eat a dinner off porcelain with silver-plated cutlery under electric light as their train sped westwards over a brand-new railway through Wiltshire and Gloucestershire.

From July 1907 the Company introduced six-day package tours of Ireland and on 16 September the *pièce de résistance* of the Irish trade – the Killarney 'Day Trips'. Actually they were 32-hour trips but the tough tourists got a full day in Killarney when, theoretically, they toured the lakes though they would probably have been forgiven if they had slept all day in the Great Southern hotel. The five-coach train, including a dining car, left Paddington at 8.40 p.m. on 16 September, driven by Driver Cock and fired by another unknown hero on the longest non-stop run up to that time on the Great Western, 261½ miles in five hours at a steady 60 mph for much of the way. They arrived on time at Fishguard at 1.40 a.m. on the 17th and were hurried on board the twin-screw, turbine steamer *St David*. In the spectacularly opulent saloon, all plush and mahogany under a heavily moulded ceiling, they tried to sleep as the ship pounded like a destroyer across the Channel at a spine-jarring 22 knots, covering the 62 miles to Rosslare in 2¾ hours. On the Irish side the best, 66-ft, clerestory carriages of the Great Southern & Western Railway were drawn up on the pier headed by a 'Kerry bogie', brand-new and raring to go. It was 155 miles, much of it over single-track lines, to Killarney and the Irish drivers went about their task with such enthusiasm that sleeping passengers were thrown out of their seats as the train swung in and out of the 'passing loops' at stations. They arrived in Killarney at 10 a.m. and had the rest of the day until 8 p.m. to explore the district before boarding the train home – and one imagines that then, even if the driver's handling of the train did throw them on the floor, they would have remained sleeping where they fell. The cold night wind on Rosslare pier would have chilled them during the short walk from train to boat, and again from the boat to the waiting train at Fishguard but when they arrived at Paddington, seven minutes early after a 956-mile round-trip they retained sufficient presence of mind to have a collection for their stalwart fireman and driver and to give them both three rousing cheers.

High quality, perfect style and first-class performance seemed to come naturally to the Great Western management after 1900 and they were not let down by their men whose loyalty, strenuous physical efforts and great skill made all this grandeur possible. Eight-, ten- or twelve-hour shifts were worked by the men according to requirements – the signalman in Reading East Main box worked eight-hour shifts while the man in, say, Thingley Junction would work ten-hour shifts, and twelve-hour shifts would be normal on the Fairford branch. Trainmen, too, worked a ten- or twelve-hour day in theory but their hours were more difficult to control and enginemen frequently worked 13–15 hours a day. In October 1904 and twice in 1907 Churchward warned the Board that his men were working excessive hours and asked for more men to be recruited. The answer was always the same: costs must be kept

down and recruitment must only keep pace with retirements or
when it became absolutely essential to take on extra men as the
result of the increasing train service. It is interesting to note
that, in February 1902, Churchward complained to his assembled Locomotive Superintendents that the engines were not as
clean as they ought to be. This may well have been a piece of
typically Churchwardian gruffness after seeing a slightly
smudged engine in the scrapyard – it hardly seems possible that
the complaint was justified. However, the Superintendents
fielded it neatly by asking if they could raise cleaners' wages so
as to encourage more boys to come forward for the work.
Nothing more was heard on the subject. Cleaners apart, the
Great Western was sought-after employment, it was a job for
life and a relatively well-paid one for even though a lad might
earn more as a butcher's boy than as an engine cleaner the
latter could look forward to a driving career and much higher
wages. In 1907 railway recruits, in general, came from school,
the armed forces or off the farms and applicants filled in a
questionnaire. 'Why do you want to work for the Company?'
Answer: 'To better myself' or – a rare, blunt reply – 'To get
more money.' Having a railway background counted for something because one question asked 'Have you any relations
working for the Company?' A separate form was sent to the last
employer asking for a 'character' and 'How much did you pay
him?' This question was almost always answered, but a Mr
Lilywhite of Ogbourne St George, who was losing his
gamekeeper to the Great Western, wrote in a big, irate hand, all
across the page, 'This question is impertinent and no business
of yours.' The gamekeeper still got his job. On the question,
'What is your opinion of his general character?' the answers
varied from the laconic, 'Worse about,' to the effusive and
scrupulously honest, 'Fred Biddle I have known all my life –
except when he was in the Army. I have always found him
willing and obliging. He knows how to do work as well as any
man in my employ and will do a good day's work anytime. I
consider him honest and industrious.' Plainly, this farmer was

loth to lose Fred but he did his best to help him and the GWR took him on in the horse provender store at Didcot where he earned 16 shillings a week in place of a man earning 18 shillings who had been sacked. Good for the Company and good for Fred who was now earning 4 shillings a week more than he got on the farm.

The Great Western paid the best rates in their own part of the country and had the pick of the men, which is why it worked so well. A career on the GWR was not to be given up lightly. A man working in the foundry at Swindon works left in March 1906 to – as he put it so loftily on his form of resignation – 'commence in business'. He went as an insurance agent, door to door, a clean, respectable job out of the heat and filth of the foundry. Sadly for him and his family the venture failed and in July he wrote to the Works Manager, William (later Sir William) Stanier asking for work and 'trusting that you will favour my application at an early date as I am anxious to get back into constant employment'. He was promptly offered his old job back. The foundry was a wretched place unless a man was as tough as a blacksmith's leather apron and the poor man wrote back to refuse the offer, saying he had found another job. If he had it did not last long for in September he wrote again, a sad, embarrassed sort of letter: 'I am writing to ask if you have a vacancy for me. I am sorry I was unable to take the place you offered me in July, I had just found employment but it was not the sort of work I cared for and the wages were not enough to keep a home in an *honest, straightforward way* (his italics). Trusting you will overlook my mistake in not taking the vacancy you so kindly offered me and will be able to give me a start at an early date.' His wife sent in her own, desperate plea, 'May I take the liberty of asking if you could see your way to employing my husband soon? As the weeks go by and every day he is seeking work without any success whatsoever I think you will understand that when a home has to be kept together it is a very serious matter.' Stanier promptly re-employed him in the relatively healthy atmosphere of the General Stores at 3 shillings a day, replacing a 4 shillings-a-day man who had been sacked. The Works, going 'hammer and tongs' to produce the superb locomotives and carriages we all admire, was not for sensitive men as Alfred Williams, the 'Hammer-man Poet', discovered. It is significant that when he complained about what seemed to him to be the ghastly working conditions in the foundry in particular and the factory in general he was ridiculed by the vast majority of men and written off by them as a 'snob'. Men walked and cycled miles to keep their job in Swindon factory and one elderly lady has assured me that her father, around 1904, walked 20 miles along the track from Steventon to Swindon morning and evening until he had saved up enough for a down-payment on a bicycle whereupon he cycled the distance daily for years.

An old driver I knew called Jack Kinch was born in Standford in the Vale in 1893, the eldest of what soon became a large and hungry family. When he was eleven he passed the school leaving examination, proving that he could read and write and had the option of staying on or leaving for work. His mother needed the extra money – he went to work. Colonel Henderson's steward at Kitemore House took him on at half a crown a week 'starving rooks' and other boy's work until he was big enough to handle a plough whereupon he became a ploughman at the bottom rate of 9 shillings a week. When Jack talked to me about those times he used steam engine slang from force of habit but the phrases applied equally to horses as locomotives. He booked on at 5 a.m. each morning to 'prepare' three horses, had them 'hooked onto the plough' at 7 a.m. and did not 'hook off' until 5 p.m. One day in the spring of 1912, when he was nineteen, he was behind his team, plodding the furrows, alone in the great, wide Vale with only the occasional glimpse of the Faringdon branch train or a far-off passer-by for company and feeling decidedly restless. The Steward rode over to see how he was getting on with the work and Jack asked, 'Don't you think I'm worth another shilling a week now?' The answer was easy, 'No.' Jack handed in his notice and the following Monday morning walked 15 miles to Swindon, making his way to the works' main gate in the hope of accosting an official. He found a fair number of other men on the same errand but managed to catch, all to himself, a bowler-hatted man dressed in black and looking very important with a length of gold chain across his waistcoat. Jack asked for a job and found himself cleaning engines in the shed. He had stopped Henry Robinson, a Locomotive Inspector, and thus accidentally began a 45-year career on railway engines – something he had not even dared to hope for.

Harry Keen, a slightly built but very energetic lad started work at Slough, straight from school, aged fifteen, in 1905. His immediate boss was a foreman whose iron face was adorned with a droopy, black moustache. He wore an elegant frock coat over a double-breasted jacket and a stiff, high collar and cravat. From these fine clothes protruded the horny hands and size 12 hobnailed boots of a strict disciplinarian whose hobby was preaching in a local Methodist chapel on Sundays so he could lay down the law on duty and off. He did his best to keep everything under strict supervision but not so strict that Harry could not slip off into Slough East box on the platform end to learn the signalling routine from the signalman, Mr Herbert. After a long lifetime Harry recalled both these men vividly and such was the impression left by the signalman that he still referred to this long dead servant of the Company as 'Mr'. Leading off from the signal box was a passageway to the telegraph office where one of the clerks found time to give him some practice on the single-needle telegraph 'teaching' instrument and, as he got better at it, this clerk would arrange for a station down the line to send some messages to which Harry would have to send the correct replies. His own job was to attend to the paraffin-burning lamps all around the station: on buffer stops, at the mail pick-up/set-down point, tail lamps of certain trains and signal lamps. Dozens of lamps had to be cleaned and burnished, vessels filled, wicks trimmed, signal lamps taken out to site – six at a time – on a special, hand-held yoke. When a Windsor line slip coach arrived off the back of a down express, Harry removed the 'Long Tom' slip tail lamp, put on an ordinary lamp for the trip up the branch and put the 'Long Tom' in the brake van of the first passenger train going up to Paddington.

When he became more experienced he was sent out as lampman, covering a district bounded by Windsor and Hayes including the Staines and Uxbridge branches. Some signal arms were more than 30 ft above the rails so their lamps were winched up into place behind the coloured glass spectacle where they rested on a metal plate which could be turned to one side to allow the lamp to rise and to be lowered. At the foot of the signal post there was a horizontal handle, moving through a quadrant, which swivelled the plate through a rod up the post and close to the handle was the winch handle. What the lamp boy had to remember was the correct sequence of actions to lower the lamp. First catch hold of the winch handle and take the weight of the lamp then pull the horizontal handle to swivel aside the top rest and then allow the lamp to fall under control of the winch handle. Harry reversed the sequence only once. He pulled the horizontal handle first, the heavy lamp fell, the whirling winch handle whacked across the back of his hand, paralysing it, the lamp hit the bottom rest, shattered like a small bomb and the heavy bull's-eye glass dealt him a salutory blow on the shin.

The Great Western expected its men to work conscientiously and to be committed to the job – on twelve hours a day it was impossible to be anything else – but, on the whole, the men expected matters to be thus, they were in regular employment for life and the general standard of behaviour was very high. The higher up the ladder a man went the more was expected of him and this was usually forthcoming but in such large numbers of men there were bound to be some who succumbed either to outright villainy or whose lives became so difficult that they succumbed to the pressures. Rankers were fined, suspended from work for a day or more and, in the last resort, dismissed – a relatively rare event – but when high officials erred matters were arranged differently. There was one Divisional Superintendent, about 1900 who, perhaps, was having a regular flutter on the horses; anyhow, it was his frequent habit to go out into some remote, single-track part of his domain and borrow money from the till of some small station and instruct the man in charge to debit the money to the parcels account at his headquarters station. Later he would repay the sum into the headquarters' account. His system worked well for some time until a travelling auditor questioned the transfers, discovered what had been happening and reported to the office of the Superintendent of the Line. It was embarrassing because all Great Western officers were assumed to be gentlemen and so, to avoid the necessity of carpeting the rascal, an official circular was issued forbidding the practice. The Divisional Superintendent failed to take the hint and shortly appeared before the Superintendent of the Line to explain himself. He gave such a good performance, explaining his circumstances, emphasising that he had always repaid the money and promising never to do it again that he was let off with a 'caution'. There it would have ended but the silly man borrowed 50 shillings from a small station a few months later. He had re-paid it before he was detected but nevertheless he was ordered to retire at once and take his pension.

In 1907 the Company appointed a Mr Kateley to be their Agent in New York. They gave him the huge salary of £1000 per annum and in return he was very effective in drumming up a good deal of trade which resulted in the great Cunarders landing traffic at Fishguard. He worked from a luxury hotel in which he bought a share – necessarily he had contacts with some of the greatest firms and richest people in eastern America – he grew better known and wealthier until he was offered a Directorship of an oil company, which he accepted. He was, as the Great Western had recognised when they appointed him at a vast salary, a bright young lad but the Company did not like their employees having outside interests which could well divert their talents from Paddington's business; his Directors might have felt differently if he had asked their permission before launching into outside interests. However, he was a very good businessman. Paddington was loth to lose him so he was allowed to have other business commitments – until 1918, when he was cited as co-respondent in a New York court case. That was behaviour quite unacceptable in a Great Western officer. He was summoned to appear before the Board at Paddington and, surprisingly for a man of his means, he went. The Superintendent of the Line recommended that he be retired on his pension but after due consideration the Directors gave judgement that, 'He must be removed from his position, his salary reduced to £250 per annum and no subsistence allowance.' He was then, in the eyes of the Great Western, merely a bottom grade clerk – probably the only clerk to be the Director of an oil company.

Another Great Western man to lose his head over a lady was Driver Percy Nutman but his fate was rather different to that of the Agent in New York. He began his time on the GWR at nineteen as a cleaner at Paddington in June 1889. After working at Frome, during which time he met a girl in Shepton Mallet and married her, and at Yeovil, he became a 3rd class driver at Weymouth in September 1898. A year later he was driving passenger trains on the Portland branch with an eighteen-year-old fireman called Willis. On 18 December they set off from the Portland branch platform at Weymouth with the 6.50 p.m., rumbled straightaway over the viaduct across a creek called the Backwater and chugged steadily up a steep gradient towards the first stop at Rodway, a mile further on. Willis was busy with his fire but when he had satisfied himself on that score he looked out over the side of the little '517' class tank-engine to accustom his eyes to the dark so as to be able to spot signals for his mate. The gradient rose at 1 in 58 as they approached the station and it suddenly occurred to him that, though the engine was blowing hard from the safety-valve, speed was down to a crawl. He turned back into the cab to ask what was wrong and to his amazement there was no one on the engine with him. Percy Nutman had vanished. Willis actually panicked for a moment, then he stepped across to the driver's side, eased the regulator open to get the train into the station, brought it to a stand and jumped down to report the loss of his driver.

The line was searched but there was no sign of Nutman in the dark and it was decided to make another search by daylight. A spare driver was sent from Weymouth and he and Willis worked the last two branch trains of the day. No trace of Percy Nutman was found except for his cap on the viaduct and the general feeling was that he had fallen off the engine into the creek and had been drowned. With that he was written off and soon forgotten. Mrs Nutman, however, was not convinced and made extensive inquiries as barely noticed actions of her husband in the past now assumed meaningful and sinister proportions. In February 1900 she reported to the Shed Master at Weymouth that her husband, far from being dead, had been seen in Shepton Mallet with her, Mrs Nutman's, younger sister and this young woman had now disappeared from home. The police were informed and after six weeks of stolen bliss living as Mr and Mrs Taylor, Percy and his mistress were discovered in a village near Leatherhead where he had found work as a woodcutter. He was taken back to Dorchester where he stood trial in July 1900. He was charged with 'unlawfully and wilfully leaving an engine whereby the lives and persons of those travelling along the Great Western and South Western Port-land Joint Railway might have been endangered'. In court he admitted to jumping off the engine and leaving his cap on the viaduct the better to give the impression he had drowned and then he had given the game away by going later to Shepton Mallet to fetch his girl rather than meeting her miles away. His great love cost him six months' hard labour. The newspapers do not recall who, if anyone, was waiting for him when he emerged from Dorchester gaol.

FOUR

Emergencies and Riots

As conceived, Brunel's railway was to go from Bristol to London and, bearing in mind that he could not ignore the wishes of the City of Bath and therefore had to go along the Avon valley, his line was uncompromisingly direct – so direct that short branch lines to towns he had 'missed' sprouted like whiskers from either side of the grand trunk. When the rails extended westwards from the originating point of Bristol through a series of Brunellian designs for nominally independent companies, the routes were, again, direct – to Taunton and Exeter at the expense of heavy earthworks. However, seen from London, these routes appeared circuitous and the magic letters GWR came to be sneered at as standing for 'Great Way Round'. The great leap forward after 1900 changed all that when a number of short-cuts were built. The 19¾-mile 'Somerton cut-off', west from Castle Cary where the line turned south for Weymouth to the old line at a place called Cogload, 4¾ miles east of Taunton, for example, was opened for passenger traffic in July 1906 to reduce the rail distance between Paddington, Taunton and points west by nearly 20 miles. Many new jobs were created for porters, platelayers, clerks and signalmen. Stations were opened at Keinton Mandeville, Charlton Mackerell, Somerton, Long Sutton, Pitney, Langport East and Athelney with their signal boxes, and two signal boxes without stations at Curry Rivel and Cogload junctions. Traffic was at first sparse, almost all of it long-haul express passenger and freight with only a trivial service locally consisting of a steam rail-car shuttling between Taunton and Castle Cary and pick-up freight for the lonely little stations threaded on the steel rails through the Somerset fastnesses.

The line was meant as a short-cut and came to life at certain seasons when summer holiday or special excursion trains ran. On Saturday 1 September 1909, Arthur Pike booked on in Keinton box at 6.20 p.m. to work through to 5.20 a.m. on Sunday when he would switch the box out of circuit until 7.30 a.m. on Monday. The weather was 'fierce cold' with six inches of snow on the ground, a very hard frost and the occasional snow-shower out of a pitch-black, star-spangled sky. Arthur laid a length of carpet along the cast-iron treads of the lever frame to keep out some of the freezing draught, stoked his tiny, cast-iron stove and settled down to signal trains through the long night. Coming down non-stop for Exeter was the 12.55 a.m. (Sunday morning) Paddington to Plymouth return excursion formed with ten corridor coaches hauled by 2923 *Saint George* in the hands of Driver Symons and Fireman Harry Elson. They tried to ignore the cold and did all right until they were passing Lavington, 87 miles from Paddington, when the pipe carrying water to the left-hand injector froze solid. Elson turned to the right-hand injector, manipulating its controls with a fervent prayer; it worked and he settled down to his firing again. The miles reeled by, Elson kept at his fire, using smaller loads per shovel, glad to be able to keep moving while his mate, huddled in his greatcoat, with newspapers tied around his legs, stood motionless, watching the pin-prick signal lamps appear out of the darkness. At 3.48 a.m., *Saint George* roared past Keinton box, Arthur Pike peered keenly from his window to catch a glimpse of the tail lamp as the rear of the train fled past in a whirling cloud of snow. There – a glimpse of red. He went to his bells, sent 2–1 beats to Castle Cary and 2 beats to Somerton, Charlton Mackerell having switched out at 8.30 p.m. on Saturday. Somerton was nearly six miles away and when the train had not cleared there at 4 a.m. Arthur telephoned his mate Bob, at Somerton, to ask if he knew where the train was – a polite way of finding out if his mate had dozed off and forgotten it. Bob had not forgotten, the train was not in sight and he had been on the point of phoning Arthur with the same question.

The 12.55 Paddington had come to a stand at Charlton Mackerell with both injectors on *Saint George* frozen. The second injector had failed just as they were rattling through Keinton and they had brought the train to a stand at Charlton to be within the protection of signals to be handy for a telephone if the need arose – and to brew tea with fresh water while they sorted out the injectors. They found the signal box in darkness and locked with all the signals in the 'clear' position. In the starry darkness, the silence of the vast fields of Somerset broken but by no means filled by the roar of steam from *Saint George*'s safety-valves, miles from help and with no way of getting water into the boiler, two grown men felt just a little lonely. One kneeling on the footplate, carefully lowering a level shovel full of blazing coal to his mate on the ballast, they tried to thaw the ice. They heaped coals on metal, they held burning coal beneath the injector, they set fire to cotton waste wrapped around the hoses – all to no avail. After twenty minutes they gave up and faced the fact that they were stuck without any rapid means of summoning assistance. *Saint George*'s boiler was full, they could close the fire dampers, close down steam to the train and preserve for some time the water it contained, but Harry Elson would have to walk to a signal box to raise the alarm. Keinton was two miles behind them, Somerton almost four miles ahead and they were right outside a closed signal box full of telegraphs and telephones. Not for the first time nor the last did an engine driver swear and wish that locomotivemen were issued with signal box keys.

They were exactly half-way between Westbury and Taunton and an engine off Taunton shed could run back to them from Somerton, up the down main, and take them on to Taunton without further fuss. If rear-end assistance was summoned from Westbury through Keinton box there would be further delay as the crippled train was pushed slowly towards Taunton with an engine in the rear. The decision was made. Symons climbed onto his engine and after warming his numb hands in front of the fire he wrote out Wrong Line Order 'B', working by the light of the furnace to complete the permit and safety certificate to the driver of the assisting engine – and to the signalman at Somerton – to allow an engine to move on the 'wrong line' towards the crippled 2923. Written on paper pink as the driver's chapped hands the 'Order' requested and promised thus: 'Allow an engine to proceed in the wrong direction to my train which is stationary at Charlton Mackerell. I will not move my engine in any direction until the arrival of the engine.' He signed it and handed it to Harry Elson, who set off at once into the snowy darkness towards Somerton.

Five minutes after he set off, at 4.25 a.m. the 10.48 p.m. (Saturday) Paddington to Kingswear express freight – 'C' headlights, fully vacuum-braked – arrived at Keinton and was unable to go any further because the section ahead was occupied by the excursion. Harry Elson struggled valiantly through the snow, running whenever the drifts allowed, only too well aware that, large though 2923's boiler was, its supply of water could not last for ever and if it dropped too low Symons would have to throw the fire out. At 5.10 a.m. he stumbled, exhausted and suffering from exposure, into Somerton signal box, fell into a chair hastily vacated by the signalman, explained the situation and handed over the Wrong Line Order. Bob hurriedly informed Arthur Pike and then telephoned Taunton locomotive shed for a fresh engine. The reply was immediate: 'None to send.' Spare engines had already been requisitioned for other failures.

'And the bloody nuisance of it is', said Arthur, when his mate told him the news, 'that we could've used the 10.48 here but for 'ee issuing that Wrong Line Order. That fireman'll have to take the Order back to the driver and we can put this yer vackum in be'ind 'im.' The Somerton signalman glanced at Elson, flaked out in the chair and taking no interest in the conversation. 'He's all done up, Arthur – can't expect 'ee to walk back out thur.' Harry Elson looked up from his reclining position. 'You can count on that. My feet and legs are soaked and I'm frozen. Why don't we just throw this bit of paper in the fire and let the vacuum in behind?' Somerton put it to Keinton. 'Tis breaking all the rules, Bob,' began Arthur doubtfully yet with a rising note of hope in his voice that it would be a way out of a very difficult situation. 'Hold on a minute, I've got the driver of the vackum 'ere – I'll ask him if he'd go.' Driver Hayes was willing after he had spoken to Harry Elson who promised faithfully that the Wrong Line Order had been burnt so that the way was in fact – if not in law – clear for the goods train to enter the occupied section for the purpose of pushing the failed train through to Somerton.

Sam Hill, guard of the 12.55 Paddington, had been protecting the rear of his train against any chance of a collision since soon after 4 a.m. He had walked back threequarters of a mile towards Kineton, showing a red light and placing detonators on the rail at quarter-mile and half-mile points and three at the threequarter-mile point where, after 1½ hours, he still stood, frozen to the marrow, hopelessly waiting for Symons to call him in on 2923's whistle. The first emotion he felt when he heard the steady beat of the goods train approaching from Keinton was alarm. He had not authorised any movement from the rear so it must be a signalling error. Then the realisation quickly followed that the engine was working very cautiously – obviously there had been some change of plan, help was at hand and, frozen to the marrow, he was not too worried about fulfilling all the formalities. He walked towards the train, holding up his red lamp, the headlights appeared, yellow-white and flickering with the engine's slow beat, he stopped it, climbed thankfully on board and began to guide Hayes to the rear of the excursion.

Driver Symons, huddled on *Saint George* in icy winds, was almost comatose with the cold and growing hunger when the triple crack of the threequarter-mile shots going off startled him awake. 'What the Hell!' He darted his head out of the cab, looked back, strode to the fireman's side and listened, ears straining, and then relaxed. Whatever was happening it was not going to end up with a rear-end collision. Something was coming very gently. Bang! The half-mile shot. He got down and walked back. Driver Hayes brought his engine to a tactful stand a few feet short of the coaches and Symons climbed up on the '43' class engine to see what was going on. He needed a lot of reassurance before allowing Hayes to couple-up and push the train forward. He had, after all, issued that Wrong Line Order and theoretically there was a danger of a head-on collision with an assisting engine but in the end the sheer cold and desperate need to make a move forced him to agree so he allowed the '43' to be hooked on. The brake-pipes were connected so that Driver Symons on 2923 would be in charge of the brake when Hayes moved the trains.

The ancient little town of Somerton woke at 6.15 that morning to the sound of a Churchward '43' as it pushed/pulled 800 tons up the grade, round the long curve, into the station. As his engine was pushed through the bridge at the eastern end of the platforms, Symons saw the lights of a locomotive standing on the up main line, realised that it must be an assistant engine for his train and gently applied the brakes. Hayes eased his engine's effort and Symons brought the composite train to a stand clear of the cross-over so that the fresh engine could 'come on top of him'. The engine had arrived from Taunton barely five minutes before so time had been saved by breaking the rules. Driver Symons fervently hoped it would be sufficient to placate Authority. The signalmen and drivers made out their written reports, emphasising the difficulties of the decisions that had had to be taken in the darkness and communication-less winter night – Taunton being unable to supply a fresh engine, the need to save 2923's boiler from burning, the exhaustion of Harry Elson. With considerable apprehension regarding the frame of mind of the Superintendent who would read their words in the well-lit comfort of his office the men sent the letters off, consoling themselves with the thought, 'What else could we have done?'

The rules had indeed been very seriously broken yet common sense was on the men's side, and, indeed, time had been saved. The Divisional Superintendents of the Traffic and Locomotive Departments were undecided: was it to be the spirit of co-operation and common sense or the Letter of the Law? They passed their responsibility to Mr Churchward and he passed it to the Superintendent of the Line, Joseph Morris. The judgement was handed down. The men had acted with the utmost good sense and had displayed commendable caution in their impromptu arrangements and were to be congratulated on their initiative.

On Sunday 10 October 1910, Driver Edward Ash and Fireman Bill Dennis had 3433, an unnamed 'Bulldog' class 4–4–0, on the 9 a.m. express from Bristol to Paddington. They arrived at Bath on time but lost ten minutes picking up a horse-box from the middle road and Eddie Ash set off determined to pick up time. The echoes of 3433's exhaust, rebounding off Bath's limestone walls made a sound as if the train was 'double-headed'. It accelerated as if it was 'double-headed' and Bill Dennis plied his shovel with a will as the engine forged its way thunderously through the serpentine curves of the Avon valley, the corrugated commotion at the chimney a measure of his own effort. They stormed through Box station doing well, Bill had her on the mark, Eddie Ash felt her pulling and felt happy. At Mill Lane Halt he turned his head for a quick glimpse of Box village and saw the neat, grey houses surrounded by their silent, Sunday morning gardens, then the cutting sides rose high on each side and the black mouth of the tunnel waited to swallow the train. Eddie pulled down on the whistle chain as they rocketed inside. 'We'll pick up five minutes by Chippenham,' he thought. Ten seconds later the driving wheels lost their grip on the rails, in spite of 17 tons bearing down on each and went into an 800 horsepower spin. Driver Ash's reactions were trigger-quick but he could act only after the event. The fierce but ordered roar of the exhaust exploded into screaming anarchy and for a fraction of a second one of the wildly spinning wheels became welded to the rails; the left-hand coupling rod sheared its crank-pin from the wheel and flailed it thunderously in the echoing darkness against the engine's framing; the right-hand rod bent and locked the wheels; and the engine came to a violent halt half a mile inside the pitch-black, smoke-filled tunnel.

As if this sort of thing happened every Sunday morning the two enginemen went immediately into action. Eddie dismounted on the off-side to make sure they were not obstructing the down line and, with the boiler water gauge lamp, looked for damage to 3433 while Bill Dennis groped on the tunnel wall for the 'tell-tale' wire which he snapped so as to sound the warning bells in Box and Corsham signal boxes. The signalmen were instantly on their feet, exchanging 'Obstruction Danger' bells before switching off the 'tell-tale' warning bell, entering the time in their registers and then going to the telephone to discuss what they should do next. Bert Wallace at Box station box, was alone except for a cleaner in the bank engine shed at the west end of the station and George Bowden at Corsham had a shunter on duty, Sid Oliver, who was duly sent into the tunnel to examine the line and bring back information.

Driver Ash, Bill Dennis and the guard of the train, John Poole, held a conference on the footplate of 3433. The engine would need the breakdown vans, preferably from the front or Swindon end, the coaches would have to be drawn back to Box station by the bank engine which could then work them eastwards as soon as the down line had been converted into a temporary single line for 'either direction' running. The passengers had been shaken by the rough stop and some were very nervous at being inside the tunnel. So, although it was against the rules, it was agreed it would be best if John Poole stayed on the train to reassure his passengers while Bill Dennis ran back to Box, putting down the detonators as he went but leaving no one standing on guard threequarters of a mile to the rear of the train. Bill arrived at Box at 10.5 breathless from running most of

the way and told Bert Wallace the situation. The 'Obstruction Danger' was then removed simply by sending 2–1 on the
bell though the 'Train on Line' indication remained pegged on
the up line indicator. The bank engine was not at Box, it had
gone through to Chippenham assisting, from the front, the
overloaded engine of an excursion train. Yet it had been gone
for so long that Bert expected that it must soon return, and they
could start to get matters sorted out. In the meantime he sent
Bill Dennis to the engine shed saying, 'Fetch young Len out of it
– he can run into the village and call Mr Chedcock', referring to
the Box Station Master. The Box banker, 4–4–0 No 3540, arrived at Corsham at 10.10. George Bowden informed its driver
what had taken place, told him to go into the tunnel carefully,
to stop and make arrangements with Eddie Ash and report to
Box. Bowden's next problem was to contact his Station Master,
Mr Troy, who might be at home or at chapel. The chapel was
nearest and most likely so he walked up onto the street, hung
around for a minute or two and then saw a man and his wife
walking towards him into the town. George stopped them, told
them what had happened and asked if they would take the
message to the chapel and the pair bustled off greatly excited to
be carrying out such an important errand.

The bank engine driver drove slowly into the murk and was
almost level with 3433 before he saw its headlights, stopped
alongside, told Eddie he would cross over at Box and come
back for his carriages and barked smartly away, arriving at Box
at 10.20. Bill Wallace pulled the points to cross 3540 to the up
line and went out onto the platform with the Wrong Line Order
'D' – Signalman to Driver – which permitted the driver of 3540
to return on the wrong line with the coaches. Young Len and
Bill Dennis went on the engine and the little 4–4–0 went briskly
away up the line, dropped Len off for Box at Mill Lane Halt and
went cautiously on towards the great tunnel, exploding the
shots as they went. John Poole, alerted by the explosions, got
onto the track and walked back to meet the engine, climbed
aboard and guided it carefully onto the rear of his train. By 11

a.m. the carriages were standing in Box station with 3540 at their head. Nothing more could be done until 3433 was cleared from the up line or the down road was converted to single-line working. Mr Chedcock, who had come hurrying from his Sunday morning newspaper, was ready to act as handsignalman at the cross-over, to clamp the points when passenger trains ran over them. Mr Troy, however, was at Corsham in a very bad mood having come helter-skelter to the station from the chapel in response to a message summoning him to what sounded like the worst train crash in history. He was waiting for a down train on which he could ride to Box to deliver the special certificate which would permit the start of single-line working.

While the coaches were being drawn back to Box, Bill Dennis was walking through the tunnel towards Corsham with Sid Oliver, carrying with him Wrong Line Order 'B' so that the breakdown vans could 'come on top of' the crippled engine, travelling down the up line. He put a detonator on the rail 150 yds ahead of the engine as a marker and walked on as briskly as possible, arriving in the gloomy, rock cutting at the east end as the breakdown vans arrived from Swindon, running under 'A' (express) headlights. The 'vans' with a large crew of men, guided by Bill Dennis, went back into the tunnel on the wrong line till the engine exploded the 'shot' – an appalling bang, echoing back three times three – taking everyone by surprise and making some men swear with fright. Fifteen minutes behind the vans was the 9.20 a.m. Paddington to Plymouth passenger train. It was stopped by George Bowden who explained matters to its driver. Mr Troy climbed onto the engine and the train set off gingerly into the smoking blackness, creeping along for fear of knocking down a workman, frequent warning whistles screeching like a thousand banshees in the impenetrable dark. While this was going on the workmen were sawing through the damaged connecting rods on 3433 and were towing it out as the 9.20 went down, the lights of the carriages flashing on the two engines, coupled head to head. Mr Troy was eventually set down at Box and was stumping bad temperedly up the signal box steps when George Bowden phoned Bert Wallace. 'That's it then,' he boomed cheerfully, 'they've just shown up out of the tunnel, they'll be on their way soon. We shan't need old Troy after all – I wager he'll be pleased!'

The Great Western had a loyal, skilful workforce, managed by the ablest of men all the way to the high-calibre businessmen of the Board. Unfortunately, for all concerned, the Board had come to take their servants' loyalty and patience rather too much for granted. The Great Western Directors recognised no trade union though they would always meet and discuss matters with deputations from the staff, those deputations being formed by trade union members. Indeed, on a slightly lower level, Churchward always urged his Locomotive Superintendents to meet deputations as quickly as possible to hear their complaints and try and sort things out 'as this would save a lot of trouble in the long term'. Churchward had also warned about the excessive hours his men worked. There had been a claim for 'milage', where men would be paid extra for driving more than 150 miles. Since 1889, they wanted 'time and a half' for Sunday work and Bank Holidays, an eight-hour day, a guaranteed week and a pay rise.

In 1907 the Prime Minister, David Lloyd-George, set up 'Conciliation Boards' to settle such claims but they soon became known as 'Lloyd-George's Confiscation Boards' and in four years achieved nothing. Great Western wages had been high relative to other manual work though hours remained very long for most men, 12–15 hours being common for enginemen in particular. The locomen had had no pay rise since 1879, other grades' wages had risen and fallen and risen again over the years, food prices had risen 20 per cent between 1870 and 1911, so that reform was overdue and the threat of a strike hung heavily. In the summer of 1911 the Great Western tried to head their men off with a very small pay rise but there was far more at stake than a few pennies extra and at 5 p.m. on a swelteringly hot 17 August 1911 the railway unions declared the first ever national railway strike. For the Great Western, at least, the upheaval was so unnecessary. The Directors were some of the most honourable, most influential men in Britain; they had been warned repeatedly by their most senior officers that the men were overworked; the Company was the second most prosperous railway in the land (after the LNWR), the work-force were the salt of the earth and deserved better treatment.

In calling the strike the unions were merely catching up with their members, many of whom had already been on strike for days, especially in Scotland and northern England. The miners were out, the engineering workers were out and the Government were now extremely worried with the emergence of this 'triple alliance'. There had been increasingly violent unrest in Britain for more than a year. In Hull, after striking dockers had refused to accept the settlement negotiated by their unions, women tore off their clothes and ran half-naked through the streets smashing windows just like a scene from the French Revolution. In Cardiff, riots during a seamen's strike led to thirty-one people being charged with offences ranging from assault to arson and attempted murder. Seen in context, this widespread strike of the most important workers in the country was very dangerous and even more so when one recalls that Britain was then on the brink of war with Germany over the Agadir 'incident'. Without railways the army could not be mobilised, without coal the Royal Navy was impotent and without engineering workers no new war machines could be made. No wonder, then, that Lloyd-George declared on 17 August: 'The Government will protect the railways at whatever cost. The whole food supply of the community, its very way of life, depends on the railway service.' The Home Secretary, Mr Winston Churchill, put this into practice by placing the army on alert with sentries armed with rifles and fixed bayonets at stations and signal boxes while cavalry patrols clattered through the streets of many towns.

Not all Great Western men could bring themselves to strike against the Company and in the great ledgers recording each man's career a black 'L' or 'D' appeared to indicate if the man was 'Loyal' or 'Disloyal' and in some cases additional information was recorded such as 'Remained in engine shed throughout. Meals brought in. Rendered splendid service', or 'Disloyal. Gave an open-air address and made himself very prominent.' This man was shortly promoted to Foreman which may or may not have a special significance. At Llanelli, a tin-plate and copper-smelting town on the edge of the Welsh coalfield, the 535 railwaymen were determined to make the strike work. The railway was at ground-level and Llanelli station stood between two level-crossings, the perfect place for a blockade of the South Wales main line and with a picket of well over 1000 men – including miners and off-duty metal workers – the crossing gates were captured and held shut against the trains, Signalman Bevan from Llanelli East box being one of the organisers. With the addition of inquisitive onlookers there were perhaps 3000 people around the gates and the railway station while the police force mustered less than eighteen men. Three trains were held up through the sweltering night of 17/18 August including the up boat train from Fishguard, the 'Cork Express', which had been able to leave the harbour only after some of the 200 soldiers on board – who had just come from Ireland – cleared pickets from the line at the point of the bayonet.

At 7.30 a.m. on the 18th 120 men of the North Lancashire Regiment arrived by train from Cardiff and tried, without success, to clear the crossings, the crowd resisting firmly and good-naturedly. When the soldiers had been repulsed the Strike Committee offered to allow two trains a day to pass provided the power of the Committee was recognised by a picket being allowed to travel on the engine. The Great Western haughtily refused such conditions and stalemate ensued. At this point two local shopkeepers, Jones and Neville, who were also magistrates, overcome by this unprecedented disobedience to Authority, sent the following telegram to Winston Churchill: 'Troops unable to cope with mob. Desire augmentation of force by nightfall.' The message was forwarded to

General Macready who blamed the situation on the magistrates for not getting in touch with him sooner and promptly
sent 250 men from the Worcestershire and the Devon regiments
to pacify a 'mob' which actually consisted of a large crowd of
cloth-capped and straw-boatered men standing around chat-
ting to the few police and soldiers at the crossings.

Some trains had been stuck at Llanelli for twenty-four hours
and the passengers, especially the women and children, were
suffering from hunger and the sheer exhaustion of waiting,
doing nothing. When the Worcesters and Devons arrived the
Great Western and the police came to a provisional arrangement with the Strike Committee that a certain number of trains
be allowed to pass but when this was put to a vote of the army of
people on the crossings it was howled down whereupon the
Worcesters and Devons moved in and cleared the gates. It is
important to note that the total staff of the railways in the
Llanelli area amounted to 535 and there were five or six times
that number around the crossings, many of them off-duty
workers from the copper-smelting and plate-rolling factories
who were not, in fact, on strike at all.

From tea-time on the 18th to noon on Saturday 19th, thirty
trains passed slowly through Llanelli subjected to occasional
stone throwing and at 1.15 p.m. Colonel Freeth advised
Whitehall that 'the strikers are under control, the trouble
comes from the tin platers not the railwaymen who are trying to
maintain order'. At 2.30 p.m. a large group of men coming off
shift from the copper works saw a train slowly passing over the
western crossing, there was no police or military guard on the
engine so it was boarded, the crew thrown off and the train
immobilised in the cutting west of the station. This brought
Major Stuart with a magistrate, Henry Wilkins, and eighty
soldiers running along the track. The workmen scrambled up
the cutting side so that when the soldiers arrived they were
rather trapped, in single file, with their backs to the carriages
and were immediately caught in enfilade by a barrage of stones.
Major Stuart climbed through the flying rocks and successfully

persuaded the men to stop throwing but as soon as he had returned to his men one was knocked unconscious by a flung stone and more followed. Henry Wilkins shouted out the statutory Riot Act proclamation: 'Our Sovereign Lord the King charges and commands all persons assembled immediately to disperse themselves and peaceably to depart to their habitations or lawful business upon the Pains contained in the Act.' Major Stuart pulled out his watch, called to those at the top of the bank that they had one minute to disperse and ordered his men to load. Rifle-bolts rattled all along the file, someone was clumsy, a single shot was fired and the nervous soldiers fired five more shots before Major Stuart could regain control. At the top of the cutting one man fell dead with a bullet through his throat; another was shot through the hand; the rest fled.

The dreadful news spread like the Plague and soon a furious crowd was besieging the station, throwing ballast stones and jeering at the soldiers within. The forces of Authority were outnumbered and, one imagines, not a little shocked.

The very presence of an excited, highly emotional crowd attracted more people, groups roamed the tracks at will and at 5 p.m. a down train was stopped opposite the sidings packed with trucks, some distance from the station. So threatening did the crowd appear that the driver panicked and tried to escape by reversing his train but his engine was boarded, he and his fireman evicted. Excitement turned to triumphant feelings of revenge when the mob discovered that they had captured the food, blankets and clothing of the soldiers penned into the station. The unprotected train was thoroughly looted and ultimately smashed-up in an orgy of hatred till the carriage doors were wrenched from their very substantial brass hinges. Without any check from the Law the riot spilled over into the sidings, wagons were broken open and their contents removed. Sides of bacon, barrels of butter, and sacks of flour were carried or wheeled away while women changed into new clothes in the yard and dressed their children in stolen coats several sizes too big. As the sultry, summer evening faded into night fires were started – using the wooden wagons – a wagon-load of whisky was discovered and the hard-working looters continued their task by firelight to the accompaniment of drunken renderings of 'Sospan Fach'. The army and police did not move into the yard until 10 p.m. by which time an exploding gunpowder wagon had killed the man trying to get into it and the riot had spread to the town. The police station and the homes of the magistrates were under attack; the windows of the shops they owned, along with most other shop windows, were smashed and the contents looted. One man, coming out of a warehouse loaded with groceries, was flattened by a sack of sugar thrown from an upstairs window of the same building! Only when reinforcements arrived in the form of the Sussex Regiment at midnight were the Authorities able to make a start on pacifying the town. In spite of several charges by soldiers using their rifles with fixed bayonets to inflict serious injuries on the rioters it was not until 2 a.m. on 20 August that the situation was under control. By then news had filtered through that, as a consequence of those very events taking place in Llanelli, the strike had been abandoned.

The strike gained nothing and the Great Western lost ninety-six wagons through fire or vandalism and dozens of carriages wrecked for a total cost of £2713 which had to be found by the ratepayers of Glamorganshire. The railwaymen's strike had been 'exploited' by others and it is to the credit of the Great Western men that they had tried to keep order during the madness of those frightening twenty-four hours.

FIVE

Railwaymen in the Great War

In March 1911 a strong, bright, sixteen-year-old called Jim Honey had joined the Great Western as an engine cleaner on Oxford shed and just two years later was sent to Llantrisant to take his promotion to fireman 3rd class. He was put to work on a 'Buffalo' class 0–6–0 saddle-tank 734 the regular driver of which was Frank Evans. Together they worked shunting jobs and lowly trips to and from local collieries. It was a rough place after Oxford and it was not long before they found themselves obliged to go on strike in a local action not recognised outside the district. Trains continued to run but one was stopped by pickets at Llantrisant and the unfortunate enginemen thrown into the river Ely hard by the station. Frank Evans would have found the strike irksome. He was fanatical about 734 and fussed over it continuously while on duty and in his off-duty time he haunted the shed, working on the engine to ensure it was in perfect order. When it was 'stopped' for its fortnightly boiler wash-out he hovered around, making sure that the washers-out did a thorough de-scaling job on the tubes and keeping the axle-boxes well protected from the torrents of water used in such work. If it had been possible he would have taken it home with him at the end of each shift.

Jim Honey was an exceptionally able, intelligent lad – those who knew him as a driver said that, had he been born forty years later, he would have gone to University and become a doctor or a lawyer. He was keen to learn and keen to do his best for 734. He and Frank got on very well and Jim was soon invited to lodge at the Evans' house. When, in 1914, 734 was taken away from Frank for some reason, he was so badly hurt that he left his wife and family, emigrated to Argentina and became a driver on the Buenos Ayres & Pacific which was, for all practical purposes, a British railway. Jim continued to lodge with the Evans (indeed he remained in contact with the daughters throughout his long life) and to work from Llantrisant shed until the outbreak of the Great War.

Following the Slough crash of 1900, the Company's engineers equipped most of their engines with a vacuum brake-cylinder and added the 'Direct Action' valve to the brake-cylinders of every vehicle. The 'DA' valve opened to allow air into the brake-cylinder in proportion to the driver's application so that the brakes were applied much faster than if air had to travel to the cylinders merely through the train pipe. The Great Western vacuum brake was, by 1904, as powerful and fast-acting as the more expensive compressed-air brakes used by the London, Brighton & South Coast Railway and the Caledonian Railway. In January 1906 a further refinement to the braking system was installed for trial on the double-track Henley branch – the marvellous, Automatic Train Control (ATC) or Audible Signalling, as it was at first called. A 44-ft-long, slightly whale-backed ramp, laid between the rails, was electrically live or dead depending on whether the distant signal to which it was connected was showing 'All Right' or 'Danger'. A contact shoe on the engine swept the ramp and caused an 'All Right' bell to ring in the cab or a 'Danger' siren to wail and the brakes to be automatically applied until the driver switched off the device and took over the braking for himself. The system worked so well that it could bring a train weighing 300 tons, with steam on to run at 70 mph, to a stand in 900 yds. In November 1908 the ATC ramps were installed between Reading and Slough and were laid through to Paddington in 1910. The reduction in nervous strain for drivers trying to run at full speed through a Thames Valley 'pea-souper' fog was enormous as the ATC bell rang cheerfully off each distant signal at 'All Right' or warned them with a siren when the invisible signal stood at 'Danger'. There were snags, however. On 6 March 1914 the fireman of a 'Star' class 4–6–0 on the 8.30 a.m. from Plymouth used the tender's water-scoop to pick up water off Aldermaston troughs as the train swept over them at 65 mph. He wound the handle round to lower the scoop, wound it back when the tender was full, and went back to firing his 'Star', 350 tons in tow and 45 miles left to do on their non-stop run to Paddington. The engine pounded on and with every mile vibration turned the well-oiled screw round and round, allowing the scoop to drop, little by little, lower and lower. The fireman had forgotten to put the restraining chain over the water scoop's handle.

The slow process was accelerated by the shaking over the sharply curved point-work of the Berks & Hants line junctions at Reading West Main signal box and the engine came out of Sonning cutting at 55 mph – and accelerating – with the scoop skimming the sleepers and the ramp for Twyford West box distant signal dead ahead. Thirty seconds later the 44-ft-long ramp was sliced off the sleepers and flung, javelin-like, up through the back of the tender, up through the leading end of the front van, narrowly missing the guard, and came to rest with a couple of feet of it jutting out through the roof at an acute angle. The enginemen neither heard nor felt a thing but the guard opened the brake-setter just as the train roared past an astonished signalman in Twyford West box, who, seeing water gushing from the tender, and a long, black 'something' sticking out through the roof of the front van, sent 'Stop and Examine', 7 beats on the bell, to Twyford East. For taking the perfectly normal action of 'putting the setter in' the guard of the train was awarded one guinea by the Directors.

On 14 March 1914 there was a 'near-miss' at Leamington which, in hindsight, looks as if Fate was having a practice run for some future calamity. Four tracks ran through the station, the up and down main lines flanked by loops serving the up and down platforms. An excursion train was unloading at the down platform and an express was signalled through on the down main. The excursion guard, his work done, gave 'Right Away' and without further consideration the driver started off along the loop on a converging course with the down main. In Leamington North box, Signalman Jack Caster saw what was about to happen, ran to the window and waved a red flag, bringing the excursion to a stand and causing consternation on the footplate of the express which was running through the station as the flag was waved.

Up at Oxford that year, among the many excellent men on the staff of the engine shed, was an outstanding driver – Peter Young. He had joined the Great Western at eighteen as a coppersmith's assistant at Oxford shed in January 1873 and went directly to 3rd class fireman – jumping the 'Pilot' grade – on his twentieth birthday. After a period in Birmingham he arranged a 'mutual swap' back to Oxford and became a 1st class driver there on his forty-third birthday in November 1897. He was highly respected in the shed and in the town and even today (1985) nonagenarian engine drivers who knew him recall him with admiration. He was a man who cared for others, a trade unionist who gave his spare time to instructing cleaners and firemen in the rules and mechanical intricacies of their engines so that they would pass the examinations for promotion. His wife had died after the birth of their fourth child and he had brought up the eldest son and three daughters 'clean and decent' in spite of railway work which regularly kept him away from home at night. In this he could not have succeeded without the help of his neighbours in Marlborough Road and the children, too, did all they could to help life run smoothly. He was a total abstainer and a regular attender at the Commercial Road Methodist chapel but he was no killjoy. His handsome face with large, wide-set eyes, straight nose and square chin held more than a hint of laughter even when staring directly into a camera for his formal photograph.

On the fine morning of 17 June 1914 he kissed his children good-bye as they left for school and presently set off for the engine shed, a short, well-built figure, walking briskly, his shiny, black box in one hand. He booked on with his regular fireman, Frank Wheeler, then the pair of them picked up their engine, 3816 *County of Leicester*, already prepared, and took it to the shed exit signal. Frank gave the 'bobby' in Engine Shed box the tip – '3816 for the 10.40 Padd' – they were let out onto the up middle road, drifted through the station and came to a stand at the signals at the south end. Five minutes later their train, the 9 a.m. Worcester to Paddington arrived; engines were changed; and at 10.40 they were away with six eight-wheeled carriages non-stop for Paddington 63½ miles away. Twenty-six minutes later at 11.6 they were steaming along through Purley cutting, four miles west of Reading at 60 mph.

At 11.5 a Taunton to Windsor excursion had run from the West of England line at Reading West Main box and had gone into the up platform line, a loop to the left of the up main line. At 11.6 the West Main signalman closed the points behind the excursion in the platform and 'asked the road' up the main to Reading East Main box, 770 yds away, for the 9 a.m. Worcester, Peter Young's train. George Randall, the Head Signalman at East Main, refused the road for the Worcester because the excursion was late and he wanted to 'nip it out' onto the up relief line without delay. This move would entail occupying the up main line for a few yards and he could not do that if he had already given permission for the Worcester to use that line.

The excursion came to a stand with its engine, 'Bulldog' class 3387 *Reading*, close to the platform starting signal which, being placed on the platform to the left of the engine, was hidden by the length of the boiler from the driver standing on the right-hand side of the cab. There was a flurry of activity. Bill Parr, a signal-porter working a ground lever and telephone from a hut at the foot of the platform ramp, was sent away with a message to shunters from George Randall. The Taunton-based driver and fireman of 3387, Thorn and Martin, hurried off, while Reading-based Driver Churn and Fireman Derman hurried onto the footplate. No time was spent in pleasantries, the excursion was late and if they were quick they could get away onto the up relief line before the Worcester came through – otherwise more time would be lost while they waited in the platform loop for the express to pass.

Passengers for Reading poured off; passengers for Windsor got on, watched by Guard Lewis Townsend standing by his van, the sixth of seven vehicles in the train. The Stationmaster, Mr Noble, was standing at the top of the subway steps; his assistant and Inspector Wood were standing to the rear of the last coach. At 11.8 Noble phoned West Main and agreed that the excursion should wait for the Worcester to pass and that a train from Southampton should be held at the branch home signal. He did not mention the plan to anyone else, he was just checking. At 11.9 someone along the platform called 'All right tickets' and another voice immediately shouted 'Right away the Windsor excursion'. Townsend raised his green flag and Noble, running the length of three coaches and shouting 'No – the Worcester has to go first,' finally knocked his arm down. The train made no move, the two men thought no more about the incident and Townsend, seeing that he was to be delayed further, went back to Inspector Wood to see about obtaining relief.

But up on the engine Fireman Derman had seen the green flag and had called 'Right Away' to his mate. Neither man looked out at the signals or they would have seen them at 'Danger'. They were too busy trying to get 3387 started, the engine was 'on centres' and would not move. Peter Young was 1½ miles away, coming in past Scour's Lane box with the 'back boards on', braking gently. To George Randall watching from East Main it was a perfectly normal scene. The excursion was still waiting quietly, it had not been 'rung out' by the platform Inspector, so at 11.10 he 'gave the road' to West Main and both signalmen lowered their signals on the up main. Peter Young put on steam. On 3387 Derman opened the cylinder cocks as his mate eased open the regulator, the engine moved back, compressing buffer springs, Churn heaved the big reversing lever into fore gear, saw the signals 'off' up the main, assumed they were meant for him, whistled and set off. Neither man checked the signal on the platform which was at 'Danger'. Randall heard 3387's whistle as the 'ding-ding' of 'Train entering Section' rang out from West Main. He ran to his up line levers and threw them to 'Danger' as his mate rang Parr's telephone in the desperate hope he was there. He was. '*Stop the Taunton!*' Parr ran up the platform ramp, whistling between the fingers of one hand, frantically waving 'Danger' with the other. Randall saw the excursion still moving as the Worcester came up alongside, whistling in terror, just braking in response to the signals ahead. On the platform Lewis Townsend ran after his van, jumped in and opened the brake-setter. There was no catch-point within the loop to protect the main line from a converging movement and 3387 stopped with the right-hand edge of its front buffer just foul of the up main as 3816 came up from behind running at 50 mph. *Reading* was flung away to the north while *County of Leicester* turned onto its right side, the driver's side, to slide at right-angles to the rails for 100 yds before coming to rest against the parapet of the Caversham Road bridge.

No passengers were badly hurt, the guilty driver and fireman were only a little shaken but Frank Wheeler took such a beating and was so badly shocked that he never worked a fast train again but remained on branch work and slow freights. Peter Young was killed and his children came home to an empty house. His blameless death was keenly felt in Oxford and hundreds of townspeople came to line the route of his funeral from Marlborough Road to the chapel. They were all in their Sunday best and the men doffed their hats as the flower-decked hearse, drawn by two black horses, passed by. Behind this came four horse-drawn carriages with his family and on foot behind were twelve retired engine drivers, the Locomotive Inspectors and Foremen of Oxford, Didcot and Swindon, followed by 350 railwaymen, two by two – almost the entire staff of the Great Western and London & North Western stations in Oxford in a column half a mile long. Sudden, violent death was, in June 1914, an unusual and terrible event.

When war was declared on Germany at midnight on 4 August 1914 cloth caps and top hats flew skywards together on the tumultuous cheers of the temporarily classless crowd beneath. In Trafalgar Square such scenes had not been seen since the night that the news of the Relief of Mafeking came through – and thousands rushed to join up, clamouring at the recruiting offices, fearful of missing the Fun with the Hun which would be over – to the latter's disadvantage – by Christmas. During August 7952 Great Western men successfully volunteered for the Colours but many more could not immediately find a place. A Railway Operating Company was raised at Paddington for the Royal Engineers' Railway Operating Division (ROD). Thousands volunteered, including Jim Honey far away in South Wales, but the ranks were filled without going beyond the Paddington area and Jim remained at Llanelli for a few more days until he heard that four regiments of artillery were being raised by a Colonel Hammersly in Oxford, whereupon he rushed home, signed on in the 135th which was to be equipped with heavy guns and was billeted in Exeter College until the full muster was reached. Then they all went up the road to a camp in Port Meadow, near a Royal Flying Corps training depot, where they went through their basic training in foot drill and small arms firing.

During 1915 the 135th Heavy Battery RA learned and perfected their specialist techniques at Bulford and Larkhill and finally sailed for Flanders in May 1916. With mules hauling their stores carts and traction engines pulling the big guns they marched cheerfully towards the Somme front through perfect, early summer weather to a smashed-up village where the guns were to be sited. Jim and his mates dug. They dug the guns into pits, they dug themselves into trenches, they dug their stores in, they buried telephone lines and lugged huge shells until, on 24 June, at dawn, Jim's gun, with 999 others, began to lay down the most ferocious barrage in the history of the world – so furiously concussive that the larks fell from the sky and lay stunned on the churned-up earth, so thunderous as to be plainly heard in Downing Street. Working shifts on this extended 'double-home' job, Jim fed shells to a smoking breech like shovelsful of coal to a 'City' on a Worcester 'fast'. For seven days he fired shells on the Boche trenches, on the Boche barbed wire, reaching a crescendo at seven o'clock on a beautiful summer morning, 1 July 1916, when tens of thousands of heavily laden British infantrymen climbed out of their trenches to advance against the uncut German wire, undamaged trenches and hundreds of expertly manned machine-guns. That particular slaughter went on for five months but for Jim it ended on the second day when he was relieved at his gun and told to report to the Battery Sergeant-Major's dug-out. Jim had been posted to the ROD and was required back at Longmoor camp to attend an army course in locomotive work. A sympathetic Transport Officer loaned him an artillery mule on which to carry himself and his heavy kit to the rail-head. He set out through the shattered lanes – and by tea-time he had been arrested as a deserter. Private soldiers do not ride mules and certainly not *away* from the battle. He stood bandy-legged from the unaccustomed ride in Military Police custody until they had checked his story, then they put him on a lorry bound for a railway station where he arrived in the small hours of the next day, utterly worn out and with no prospect of a train to the coast because everything was going towards the battle. What could have been a very cold, hungry wait was made bearable – memorable – by being served free tea and sandwiches from a canteen run by a 'stunner' of a girl – Bessie Boots, heiress to Boots the Chemist.

A train of wounded came in, heading for Le Havre. Jim climbed into the brake van with the Chef de Train and arrived with the smell of the sea like a promise of 'home soon' in his nose. In this frame of mind he reported eagerly to the RTO, was directed to the Headquarters of the Royal Engineers in the town, and the following morning he was on the move again – going up and down the dock sidings as fireman on a Midland

Railway o–6–o. The ROD was short of men, and he was drafted direct to the footplate without benefit of Longmoor training yet – and this really did add insult to injury – not only had he lost his trip back to 'Blighty' but his wages of half a crown a day were fourpence a day less than those he would have got if he had done the ROD course at Longmoor. Jim was promoted to driver later in 1916 but continued to work within the marshalling yards at Le Havre, Boulogne and Calais. If he had to go along the *Nord* main line from one yard to another he was accompanied by a French or British pilotman who knew the road and the *Nord* system of operating. He and his fireman worked on all kinds of British o–6–o goods engines. Some of them – as Jim said – never were any good and the lack of maintenance in France made them even worse. There were Caledonian, North British, Midland, South Eastern and South Western Railway engines and the legendary, war-proven 'Dean goods' of the Great Western. Shunting 8oo-ton trains for twelve hours a day was wearisome in the extreme, especially if an engine had missed its proper maintenance and would not therefore raise steam.

If an engine stalled in the yards the men could spend time sorting it out but if a failure occurred on the main line one was blocking an artery of supply to the Front. By mid-1916 the overloading of the British Expeditionary Force's railway engines had become serious and the Government asked the major companies for 160 o–8–o locomotives. The Great Western possessed none and their super-powerful 2–8–o engines were employed on the strategically vital trains of 'Admiralty coal' out of the Welsh coalfields north to Scapa Flow so they offered another twenty-two 'Dean goods' and twenty of their brand-new '43' class 2–6–o mixed traffic engines which, said the GWR's Locomotive Department, 'are the equal of any o–8–o in Britain'. The truth of this was acknowledged by the Government's technical advisers and the engines were sent to France.

Working the yards twelve hours a day, Jim and his fireman shared their engine and living accommodation with another set of men and towed behind the engine, when moving from yard to yard, a 'living van' after the manner of a road traction engine driver. The van was parked in the sidings and in it they slept between shifts, cooked in it, too, when they were working in one of the vast, new yards built specially for the war effort, such as the one laid out on the dunes by McAlpine's navvies at Dannes Camiers. Life was dull but safe, out of reach of German death. Jim discounted the high explosives he was constantly shunting – it was British, and therefore no danger.

Early in 1917 he was working at a vast ammunition dump which had been established on the outskirts of a town called Audrique near Calais. A small town of tents and huts accommodated the hundreds of men from various corps needed to look after the bombs and bullets. Jim and his mates had their living van, there was entertainment in Audrique if they had time off and life settled down to an almost peacetime routine. Characteristically, Jim set about the translation of the French railway rule-book into English so he could pass his examination with the *Nord* Inspector and take long-haul trains on the main lines. His studies were rudely interrupted one afternoon when the 'impossible' happened and German biplanes bombed the dump. Accuracy was unimportant, the place was huge and only a few bombs were needed to set the entire stock of ammunition into a chain reaction of explosions. The 'holiday camp' was blown apart. Men came bolting naked from their tents, terrified, all searching for some solid cover. Jim and his mates got under their engine, normally a bit of a squeeze for one man when 'oiling round' but quite roomy for four when thousands of tons of cordite-driven steel and cast-iron were flying. The dump took a day and a night to explode, the town of Audrique was evacuated and the night after the raid it was thoroughly looted by British soldiers. In the cool of the following dawn Jim watched the culprits come shame-faced home between armed Military Police escorts.

In mid-1917 Jim Honey was called to Calais to face the *Nord* Inspector on the rules governing the working of that railway. It was the strangest examination an honest Great Western man ever had; hearing the questions and giving the answers through an interpreter – a Royal Engineers officer – so that Jim never actually knew if his answers were correct. Any inaccuracy could have been made right by the officer in translation and the French Inspector would have been none the wiser. Jim struggled manfully with the Gallic railway phrases which he translated into 'Tommy' French: 'Biffer' boards, 'Rallenteer' boards, 'Advertisement' boards, 'Disc Rooge' and 'Pallet Sem'. At last, the interpreter told him he had passed. The Inspector handed him a book of gradient charts for the railways of northern France, kissed him on both cheeks as if he was presenting him with the Croix de Guerre, and a somewhat shaken Jim Honey staggered out into the streets of Calais, a fully qualified driver on *Chemin de Fer du Nord*.

His regular engine was now a Baldwin 4–6–0 recently arrived from the United States. His fireman, while not a railwayman, certainly knew all about shovelling coal – Dai was a miner from South Wales, many years Jim's senior, but they took a great liking for each other and, with the engine, formed an inseparable team for many months. They serviced their engine on *Nord* sheds and roamed the network of tracks from Le Havre to Dunkirk to wherever the Front Line happened to be at the time, each trip lasting days with small provision for food and none at all for sleep – so there was as much risk of dying from sheer exhaustion as from enemy action. Jim thought the work would be a change from the monotony of shunting and soon realised that the shunting had sent him mad, so mad as to volunteer for work where he was frequently on the receiving end of all that the German artillery could throw at him.

They would arrive at Calais with an ambulance train, the engine was serviced and they would be ordered out at once with ammunition. They were issued with rations according to how long the trip was supposed to take – a bureaucratic nicety with no relationship to reality – so that they were usually hungry. The food would go into the tool box, rifles and steel helmets up in the corner of the cab out of the way and then the long, long wait to get off the shed – never mind about getting into and out of the marshalling yard – hence some of the meagre rations would have been eaten before the job actually started. Sleep was more important than food in so far as sleep could not be stolen but, as Jim said, 'a man could only take so much'. They would use delays, when the line was blocked by shellfire or bombing, to curl up in their greatcoats on the footplate or, if the Chef de Train was 'all right', in the draught-free confines of his caboose. If they were delayed at a depot Jim and Dai took turns to sleep and stand guard against officious officers who would have been delighted to court-martial a man for 'sleeping on duty in the face of the enemy' or some such nonsense. Dai took a truly fatherly interest in Jim, made him his 'butty' and became a demon forager, able to discover 'ownerless' tins of bully beef or bottles of wine wherever they stopped. Jim would be ordered to rest by Dai and would then be woken with a poke in the belly from a long loaf of fresh French bread which the Welshman had 'liberated' along with some army cheese. They shared everything – the food and the dangers – and grew very close in the private world of the Baldwin's cab, two against bureaucracy and the officious Chef de Train.

They were stopped one day on an embankment with shellfire up the line. Dai dropped the dampers to keep the engine from blowing off steam, then they both slept until a terrific bang woke them. They were being shelled. Nothing new in that, they were out of the cab and under the tender in seconds and sat and winced as the German artillery searched for targets. Jim was just comforting Dai with the thought that the guns were at extreme range when a single shell fell into the ballast only a few feet away, scattering stones like shrapnel. They flung themselves flat and lay, hearts pounding, for what seemed an age till they realised they were still alive – a shell exploding that close would have blown them away. They raised their heads warily and saw a crater in the opposite track and on one side the black stump of an unexploded 6-in. shell.

The strafing eventually stopped, they crawled out and climbed back on the engine only to discover that the fire had gone out. There was enough steam in the boiler to work the blower, the firebox was very hot, so while Dai set off with the coal pick to find some kindling, Jim set-to with a bar and with judicious use of that wonderful American invention, the rocking grate, began to clear the clinker and ash ready to light a new fire. Twenty minutes later the sounds of an altercation reached the footplate. Dai was coming back with someone's front door in his arms and the French Chef de Train alongside shouting angrily. Unconcerned Dai handed the door up to Jim, climbed aboard and levelled his Lee-Enfield at the Chef's head. A few words of unmistakable Anglo-Saxon followed (there are no rude words in Welsh) and the Chef scrambled back to his van.

Twelve hours later they were near the dump where they would leave the train. It was just about dawn and the tail light of the train ahead was visible; there was a queue of trains waiting to enter the yard, sitting ducks for German planes or artillery. As the sun rose a mist formed and thickened and first Dai, then Jim, felt his chest tightening and his eyes smarting. They were standing on ground saturated with poison gas and the rising mist was bringing something residual off the earth. For once the two men were scared. Shellfire was a sudden whizz-bang and one was alive or dead but this was death by creeping suffocation and there was no escaping it. For two hours they sat in increasing misery, gasping for breath until the sun grew hotter and the mist cleared. Dai's lungs had already been damaged in the mines so he suffered worse than young Jim who took over firing duties leaving the relatively sedentary driving to his mate. Neither man ever thought of giving in, their loyalty to each other carried them through.

On their travels they met locomotivemen from the Empire and from Argentina, some of whom had gone out after being sacked off the Midland and London & North Western Railways for taking part in the 1911 strike. So many of these 'disloyal' men had come back from Argentina to join the ROD that they were formed into a special unit with the badge of the Southern Cross on their sleeves and 'Argentina' on shoulder-flashes. Remembering Frank Evans, Jim asked each man he met wearing the Southern Cross badge if he knew Frank and at last Jim tracked him down to a pumping station where he was in charge of some big stationary engines. They had a great, back-slapping reunion and Frank showed Jim round his pets. They were far grander than 734 but in the same pitch of mechanical perfection and turned silently without a leak of steam, every gauge and pipe burnished to perfection by the intensely enthusiastic Frank. 'You'd hardly want the war to stop,' said Jim, half-joking, half-probing. Frank gave him a sheepish grin. 'Oh, I dunno, when this lot is over I reckon I'll go back to Llantrisant.'

Jim was retained in the ROD well into 1919, working military specials from Calais to Cologne. Strictly speaking he drove as far as the border at Hervestal where a German engine and crew took over and he became their armed guard but they were locomotivemen the same as Jim – and a lot hungrier. Jim found it impossible to point a rifle at them so the Lee-Enfield stayed in the corner and he took his turn driving and firing some fine engines. It was a highly experienced ex-driver Honey who returned to Llantrisant as a fireman on a saddle-tank.

Frank Evans was already there, living at home once more and working as a shed turner, moving engines about the shed. The Great Western did not normally allow those of their servants who had resigned to return but a special case was made for Frank except that he was made to understand that he would never go out on the main line again. This knowledge was a sore trial and he shortly took another of his radical decisions by uprooting his family and transporting them to Bourne-mouth where he had bought – of all things – a horse-drawn milk round. It was a disaster. Frank was a kind father, a patient, careful man with machinery, but horses he did not understand. They were wilful, flesh-and-blood personalities, not amenable to adjustment by spanner, not capable of long hours of work.

He was successfully prosecuted twice for cruelty to his horse and after the second occasion his customers deserted him. The business collapsed and Frank, in debt, found safe refuge once more in another pumping station.

SIX

Long Shifts on the Home Tracks

At the outbreak of war there was a pandemonium of patriotic fervour, military traffic and spy scares. The railways of Britain were taken over by the Government 'for the duration', run by an Executive made up of the chief officers of the major concerns. The trade unions loyally called off a strike planned as a protest against worsening pay and working conditions. What was to befall was far worse than anything the trade union had had to complain about. In the first three weeks nearly 8000 Great Western men volunteered to fight and those who went into the forces without permission were penalised, or rather their families were to the extent that they did not receive the due proportion of the man's railway wages 'plus sixpence'. Even then it was difficult to hold the men back. The Great Western was, on the one hand, asking for recruiting posters to be patriotically posted-up in their engine sheds and on stations and, on the other hand, the men were being told 'you are serving your country just as well by staying on the railway'.

Every route was supposed to have a military guard but this was impossible so certain routes were guarded by armed sentries – Basingstoke to Reading was one – but not Didcot to Oxford, though this was later guarded. From 15 August 1914, 1200 permanent-way men were placed as unarmed sentries to guard the line against the possibility of sabotage by German agents and a soldier armed with a Lee-Enfield rifle was placed at each end of the Saltash bridge and at both ends of various tunnels including those of Severn, Evershot and Bincombe. Anyone they saw walking on the line was to be challenged and, if necessary, shot. This made life uncertain for the gangs of permanent-way men and for the solitary patrolman whose job it was to inspect the 'length' each day, so the instruction was that no one was to go on the line until the military had been advised and an armed guard provided for the railway workers. This proved tolerably impossible to comply with, the more so when autumn fogs clamped down suddenly upon the line, making the soldiers even more jittery as they could hear footsteps approaching through the murk but not see who was coming. Presumably the War Department had given their men instructions on how to repel any hordes they might find invading and the Great Western gave them strict instruction on how to conduct themselves on the track so that they would not be run over but in neither case was there any great success. Fourteen soldiers were killed by trains and two 'own goals' were scored when nervous sentries shot dead the man coming to relieve them. The whole operation was unworkable – and unnecessary – and was soon dropped.

Vital stores for the army were in short supply in those early days and GWR horses were requisitioned right out of the shafts of the carts they were pulling, the going rate for a good horse being 'cost plus 50 per cent' which seems like good business except that a replacement horse was hard to find because so many had been conscripted. Requisitioning did not always go smoothly: a GWR stable, for example, was raided by the army, three full sets of cart-horse harness were removed, and a 'fiver' left by way of recompense. That caused a terrible row and there had to be an inquiry to decide the proper price of horse collars.

Only 2012 men were taken on to replace the 7592 who had volunteered for France during the first three weeks of the war and between 4 August and 31 October the Great Western ran 3239 military specials. It was usual for twenty-six trains of 'Admiralty coal' to leave Pontypool Road for Rosyth in twenty-four hours for the entire duration of the war though these trains did not run every day of the week. Stationmasters and others in charge were told to take on women if at all possible rather than men, because women could be paid less to be porters or signalmen. Women soon became essential to the war effort when Swindon factory was, in part, turned over to the production of munitions. Staff taken on 'for the duration' were given no uniform but only a 'service' armband for those GWR men away at the war would want their jobs back after Christmas. Thus reduced in numbers the staff had to cope with a traffic far in excess of anything handled in peacetime. There were more people in work, earning better wages, more could afford to travel – more had to travel to get to work – and at week-ends and holiday times thousands queued at main stations fully expecting to find trains to take them to Henley or Torquay as if there was no war. The Great Western obliged them until after the 1916 Christmas rush when the strain on men and the depleted stock of locomotives became so great that from 1 January 1917 the Government allowed fares to be raised by 50 per cent to discourage travel while slip carriages and restaurant services were suspended, many express trains were removed and a general limit of 60 mph was placed on the remainder. The only effect was to make the remaining trains longer and heavier, crammed to the doors with people. Suburban trains also grew heavier because the small threat of German air raids on London had caused an exodus into the Thames valley. Air raids then were puny affairs but simply by appearing in London skies the planes could cause more havoc than by dropping their little bombs. In March 1918, for instance, an enemy plane flew over west London and dropped nothing but the defensive fire it drew fell back to earth and caused £80 damage to the roof of Paddington station.

The war increased the work of freight train engines and crews not only because of the vast military traffic in troops and munitions but in such obscure items as the return of wagons to other railway companies, so that all other companies' trucks had to be sent to central yards, formed into full trains and returned empty to their owning companies. At the start of the 'common user' policy in April 1916 Great Western men were so used to *not* using 'foreign' wagons that great difficulty was encountered overcoming their deep-seated prejudice – as Company minutes show. The traditional way for Admiralty coal and shipbuilding steel to travel from source to consumer was by coasting steamer but these small ships had largely been commandeered by the Royal Navy and their cargoes went across Britain by rail, through Shrewsbury to Rosyth. By the end of 1917 Great Western goods train milage had increased by 23 per cent over 1914 compared to a 3 per cent increase on the L&NWR.

The Great Western and London & North Western jointly owned Shrewsbury station where trains converged from Chester, Crewe, Paddington and the south coast towns, from Aberystwyth and Pwllheli, from South Wales via Brecon and via Hereford, from the west of England and from Worcester via the Severn Valley line. At the north end of the station, right off the platform ends, the tracks divided: northwards, straight on, for Chester; sharp right, eastwards, for Crewe. The controlling signal box, Crewe Junction, was worked by the 'three Teds' – Ward, Griffiths and Punslow – one man on duty for eight hours a day, six days a week with one Sunday off in three. They worked without a booking lad, signalling trains to and from Coton Hill South box, 550 yds north, Crewe Bank about the same distance east and Centre cabin 160 yds away along the platform. Each man carried out all the telephone work necessary to regulate trains over the junctions, in and out of the crowded station and the local marshalling yards at Coton Hill, Abbey Foregate and Coleham which were hourly full to overflowing. There were 'light engine' movements and passenger trains to be marshalled not to mention trains of fish or horses, all of them using the tracks across the junctions as a marshalling yard. All shunting moves and regulating messages, all the actual routine of signalling trains and pulling the levers for those trains, were carried out by one man. No wonder he could find time only for 'skeleton booking', recording in the register only the emergencies or the out-of-course delays.

1 Gooch 8-ft 'Singles' *Great Western* and *Swallow* at Didcot with the 5.5 p.m. Paddington passenger train *c.* 1890

2 A team of GWR platelayers slew Brunel's broad gauge into Stephenson's 'coal-cart' standard gauge, 21 May 1892

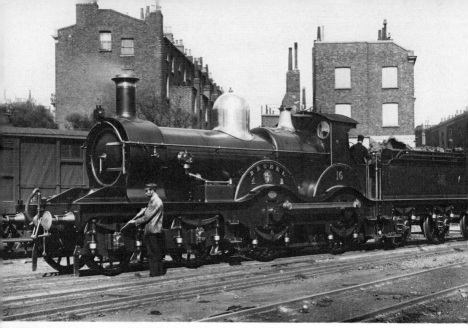

3 The New Image: 16 *Brunel* [
Paddington, *c.* 1895, the
driver obligingly posing wi[
his 'long feeder' oil can
professionally displayed

4 3297 *Earl Cawdor*, dressed u[
for the Diamond Jubilee
train of 1897, outside the
Chief Mechanical Engineer[
offices at Swindon

5 Inspector G. H. Flewellyn (*centre*) with 1873 at Exeter St David's station, 1 July 1903. The engine is decorated to work the first train over the Exeter–Christow branch

6 Passengers venturing onto the fearsome early motor buses, operated by the Great Western, reverted to stage-coach speeds, 12 mph, and to riding 'outside' or 'inside'; this is the Marlborough–Calne motor bus, *c.* 1910

7 War work on the Home
  Front. Great Western
  milkmaids take over men's
  work in the sour smell of
  bad milk at Paddington,
  1916

8 Great Western Fireman
  Jim Honey (*right*) in Royal
  Engineers' uniform as a
  Sapper Driver with his
  Yankee 4-6-0 somewhere in
  France in 1918

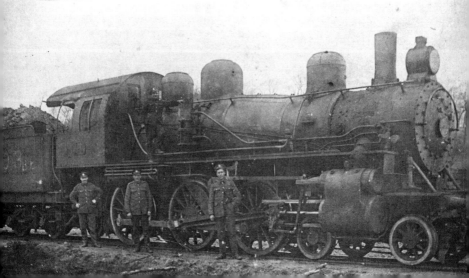

9 Ben Davies (*sitting nearest camera*) joined the GWR at Lydney the day that
the shorter (eight-hour-day) working week came into force: 1 February 1919

10 Passengers crowd around the cab of 2915 *Saint Bartholomew* at Paddington
on 9 July 1923 to congratulate Driver Hopkins and Fireman Bailey on bringing
the inaugural run of the world's fastest train into Paddington, $1\frac{1}{2}$ minutes
before time

11 During the General Strike, called in May 1926, hundreds of laymen
    volunteered to work on the railways – though no one offered to hew coal.
    At Paddington eager volunteers worked under the glum gaze of cloth-capped
    railwaymen

12 In 1929, to mark the 25th Anniversary of the 'Cornish Riviera Express', a
    new design of carriage, 9 ft 7 in. wide, emerged from Swindon works. They
    were first used on 8 July as a 14-coach set, including slip coaches, seen here
    loading heavily at Paddington

13 Weymouth terminus in 1931, destination for slip coaches off the 'Cornish Riviera Express': (*left*) a 1904 steam rail-car; (*centre*) 'Bulldog' class 4-4-0 3324 *Glastonbury*; (*right*) a Southern Railway 'T9' class 4-4-0 on a Bournemouth train

14 Super-sleek diesel rail-cars were introduced in 1933. Some were fitted with buffet facilities and performed 'Inter-City' services between Cardiff and Birmingham. This one is stopping at Taplow in 1935

15 A GWR pannier tank beneath LNWR signals and signal box at Addison Road
(now Kensington), 1935. The station was on the 'West London' line, a
strategic north/south link across the Thames

16 2568, a Dean 'Standard Goods' built in 1898, near Flax Bourton in 1939.
The single headlamp below the chimney indicates that this is a 'B' headcode,
stopping passenger train

17 Children being evacuated from London during the Second World War to live
    with families in 'safe' areas. This photo was taken somewhere on the GWR's
    London district in May 1940

18 Barrage balloons suspending steel cables were intended to protect the GWR's
    Channel Islands ferry *St Julien* from low-level air attack as she lay at anchor.
    Requisitioned by the Admiralty in 1939, as a hospital ship, the large red
    crosses were no shield against attack during the Dunkirk evacuation

19 The Second World War brought shortages of every kind. Here at Paddington in 1942 several passengers watch with apparent envy as an aged porter helps an old lady with her luggage

20 Protected by a stalwart 'look-out' man, women workers once again take over the dirty job, while the men are away at the war. Greasing the junction points in the down main line to the Newbury line at Reading West Main in 1942

21 Saddle tank engine 1729, looking as if it has been savaged by a large dog, lies where it was blown by a very near miss from a Luftwaffe bomb at Castle Cary on 3 September 1942. The cheerful soldiers are from 82 Coy, Royal Pioneer Corps

22 Brunel's roof at Paddington, still standing after absorbing a shock to its fabric never envisaged by its illustrious designer. The track, embedded in brick, has been thrown onto the platform by bomb-blast on 22 March 1944

23 February 1947 at Dowlais Top: RAF personnel wait to fire Rolls-Royce 'Derwent' jet engines to clear snow and ice, as an observer bites his finger apprehensively

24 The Great Western's Indian summer. Grimy, but full of fight, 'Castle' class 5079 *Lysander* comes storming up to Whitehall box, filling the signalman with admiration for the noble machine. The Company would soon disappear but the spirit remained till the end of steam haulage

The continuous procession of GWR and LNWR trains over the junctions, below the ancient castle, above the city streets, in and out of the great, iron-roofed station in their bright, contrasting liveries – all this comes out strongly when I turn the yellowing pages of the old registers and read the entries made, even under stress, with a neat, clear and unhurried hand – especially by the helpfully explanatory Ted Ward. The multitude of vehicles, the colourful liveries are easily conjured, the barking exhausts and shrill whistles of engines hauling 'GW Horses, Hadnall to Minsterly; LNW Horses to Swaythling; GW Troops, Manchester to Codford; LNW Sailors, Invergordon to Plymouth; GW Mules to Lancaster; Naval Ambulance (no advice received), Rosyth to Plymouth'. Admiralty coal trains coming along in convoy as near as the block system would allow, five together, troop trains, also in convoy, belled 4–4–4 or 3–2–1. It was usual for five 'light engines' to run coupled through the station and sometimes, to get them through, they would be coupled to the front of whatever train 'had the road' and was passing.

The yard at Coton Hill was always within one train of full capacity and frequently not only was the yard full but so was the goods line and the main line between Crewe Junction and Coton Hill. The signalman at Coton Hill South box was constantly telephoning back to Crewe Junction to 'put the block on' with messages such as 'No more trains till after the Zulu' being a daily ritual. Having spent many years as a signalman I can read into the entries made, in particular, by Ted Ward the annoyance he felt with his mate at Coton Hill South. Ted's notes across the page are precisely and fully worded – a defensive device to clear himself in case an official should ever inquire into the cause of a delay. On 18 January 1916 a troop train disgorged its load onto the down platform at Centre cabin and at 9.3 the signalman there sent to Ted Ward, on the 'Train Describer', the message 'Empty coaches to Coton Hill Yard'. Ted asked the road for the empty stock to Coton Hill South, the man there refused the road and, over the phone, told Ted that the coaches were for Crewe. Ted altered his levers for the Crewe direction whereupon the fireman of the erstwhile troop train came to the box to say that his mate did not know the road round to Crewe Bank. Ted wearily reversed his road again and told Coton Hill South that he would have to have the coaches because they were blocking the down platform for the 'Zulu'. Ted set the road for the loop and into that line went the coaches. Coton Hill South, though, was busy shunting and did not draw other trains out of the loop so that the coaches could not get properly 'inside' but remained with the last coach out over the points, preventing them from being closed and delaying the 'Zulu' for thirty-five minutes. I can just imagine Ted going on the phone to Coton Hill South with an irritable, 'Can't you drop one down off the loop and make some room? What the hell are you hanging about at down there?' And his opposite number giving him a dusty answer.

Heavy snow fell on 15 February 1916, blotting out signal spectacles and clogging points. At 2.30 a.m. on that bitter morning, Ted Ward sent for his 'snowmen', Messrs Stokes, Jones and Woodfin, stout of heart and leather of skin, out of their warm beds to sweep snow until breakfast at 5.30 a.m. They were finally allowed to go home at noon. Without them the naval ambulance trains, coal, bombs and ordinary passengers would not have passed through Shrewsbury. Blizzards swept across England throughout February and March culminating in a thoroughly nasty, howling gale, a hurricane of snow which sprang up on the evening of 27 March and blew most devastatingly for forty-eight hours. The Great Western's central area was affected: Newport to Chepstow and Gloucester, Newport to Hereford and Worcester (but not Shrewsbury), Gloucester to Stratford-on-Avon and Birmingham, Bicester and Oxford to Wellington (Salop). Everything within the framework of those routes was affected, the tracks were buried deep in snow and chunks were blown away by the wind. A footbridge and a half-built signal box at Margam were blown away, 1500 telegraph poles were either blown down or blown sideways, destroying 8000 miles of circuits and putting the signalling system out of action. An engine was pole-axed and severely stunned by a telegraph pole falling across its boiler. In the deep darkness of the night of 28 March an elm tree fell across the line, in the cutting, at the east end of Devizes tunnel and would have caused a crash had not a boy been struggling home at the time, heard the rending noise of the falling tree and run back a mile to the station to raise the alarm. The Great Western Directors voted him no less than three guineas.

On 27 March the 6.30 p.m. Neyland to Paddington Mail, Milk and Sleeping Car train left 'right time' behind 3303 *St Anthony*, driven by the legendary John Thomas, piloted by 3355 *St Aubyn*, two 'crack' engines from Neyland shed. They were hauling a load of nine 'eight-wheelers' including two Travelling Post Office tenders for Gloucester behind 3303. The guards were a pair of mates, well-known Paddington 'top-link double-homers' – Head Guard Campion, in the rear van, and Junior Guard Shelley riding as an assistant. All 'A' class trains ran with two guards, the Junior riding in the front van where there was one; Campion and Shelley worked together for years and were well known from Chester and Fishguard to Paddington. Throughout the long and difficulty journey which lay ahead, frock-coated Campion kept a meticulous log of the run.

At Clynderwen, first stop twelve miles from Neyland, they picked up a six-wheeled milk truck loaded with dead rabbits – the sole export of the Maenclochog branch and at Whitland Junction three passenger carriages were attached off the Pembroke line so they left a few minutes late with thirteen vehicles. Driver Thomas hated to be late and it was well known that he always tried to make up time so one may easily imagine the noise his beloved *St Anthony* and the assisting *St Aubyn* made between station stops as the two engines and their loyal firemen were hammered into speed in an effort to regain time with a very heavy train. Station work was also heavy with tons of mail and parcels to be loaded. The weather was blowing a gale, the night pitch-dark as the see-saw battle went on between the engines and the clock. Minutes lost at platforms were clawed back under a trail of fiery smoke through Carmarthenshire until they ran into the well-defined edge of the blizzard after the Bridgend stop and thereafter took fifty minutes for the twenty miles to Cardiff. Here, in full blizzard conditions, the engines were changed and the 'passenger shunters' reformed the train. The Pembroke three came off, two for Paddington were inserted behind the GPO tenders – all this entailing a lot of shunting – and, forty minutes later, the eleven-coach train left behind 3813 *County of Carmarthen* driven by Driver Mitchell. Section by section, almost signal by signal, he conned the train through the snow-thick dark, the westerly gale blowing snow onto his and his mate's back over the low tender, plastering the signal glasses impenetrably, till at last they arrived in Newport, at midnight, having covered the eleven miles from Cardiff in forty minutes. The storm was then raging so furiously that they were quite unable to proceed, the entire signalling system for miles and miles ahead had been destroyed and telegraph poles threatened to fall and block the line. Newport station was full of trains, like ships in harbour, waiting for the storm to die down.

With the first, bitter, grey light of dawn, at 7.30 a.m. on 28 March, Driver Mitchell set off with his train into a howling wilderness of snow, creeping along at 15 mph under the 'Time Interval' system, looking out for a red or green flag from each signalman, whose only control over trains was to prevent one following another by an interval of less than ten minutes. He took seventy-four minutes for the seventeen miles to Chepstow but covered twenty-eight miles from there to Gloucester in an hour. There the train was re-marshalled once again and, packed with passengers off cancelled trains, set out under normal signalling for Swindon stopping specially at Brimscombe to set down passengers. From here the line climbed steeply and most tortuously up the Golden Valley for almost four miles till it pierced the Cotswold ridge in the tunnels at Sapperton. A powerful, 2–6–2 type tank engine 3118 went 'on top' of 3813 and together they raised the echoes from Chalford to Slad, Frampton Mansell to Bisley across the snow-blanketed, deep-cleft, wooded valley. At Swindon, the mail and passenger connections from the west of England had gone on to Paddington as a 'special' so all that was needed was to carry out the booked engine change. 3813 *County of Carmarthen* was replaced by 'Saint' class 2973 *Robins Bolitho*, Driver Pocock. Guard Campion, still soldiering on, went up to the engine to give the new driver the load and to see who he was. The scheduled time was bettered by two minutes with the splendid *Robins Bolitho* and the desperately beleaguered passengers from Wales were delivered to their destination at Paddington ten hours late at 1.34 p.m. after nineteen hours on the road.

The devastation of communications was, within the well-defined and large area, complete. Gangs of Great Western telegraph linemen were drafted in from unaffected areas but they were too few and the Company was forced to ask for help from the GPO and the Royal Engineers. The GPO sent fifty miles of very special wire which was sheathed in the latest insulation and could therefore be laid along the ground to temporarily restore 'block' working until the flattened pole routes could be restored and to do this 250 sappers from the Royal Engineers were loaned by the War Office. Fifty of them were billeted on householders in Oxford – at the GWR's expense – and the rest were accommodated in coaches at various locations around the damaged area. Block telegraph working was fully restored on 7 April and a Company minute records the Official Appreciation of 'the very excellent work carried out by all members of the Company's staff'. Some men worked, literally, all around the clock to restore order; nine Inspectors were awarded £10 each, ten workmen got £5 each and two men £1 each. It was not until 3 August 1916 that the 1500 poles and 8000 miles of wire were fully restored. A Company minute records that in carrying out this work the sappers' labour was worth £6000 'had the soldiers received wages and therefore £250 is being disbursed among the soldiery' to quote exactly the quaint language of the minute-book.

Throughout the Great War thousands of men – and women, for there were women in the signal boxes and on the station platforms – worked to the limit of their endurance, even those with the secret, black 'D' on their record. This was as well for the British war effort considering that almost all the bullets, nearly all the fit soldiers and mangled wounded were transported to France and around Britain over Great Western metals. When military manpower was in particularly short supply the Great Western could always be relied upon for support. In February 1917 the Royal Engineers needed 100 extra men to lay a new railway near the front line in Flanders and 100 GWR permanent-way men volunteered overnight. They went out to a place called Steenwerck and worked fourteen hours a day for ten days to complete the job four days ahead of schedule, showing, so the Official 'thank you' letter said, 'a magnificent spirit even under shellfire'. One cannot help but wonder if the shellfire had had something to do with the lightning speed with which they had built the line. Anyhow, they had faced all hazards bravely and were back in Blighty after a fourteen-day adventure, an unrepeatable experience, and one which probably altered profoundly their ideas about the 'glory' of war.

During 1917 the Government ran short of bandages – cotton was in short·supply as a consequence of the German U-boat blockade of Britain – and asked the Great Western if they had linen suitable to be made into wound dressings. In response several thousand old plans, done on linen, were boiled and bleached free of watercolour paint and ink and the resultant acres of cloth were then cut into miles of bandages and thousands of historic records were sacrificed along with the soldiers to the God of War. Resources were being drained into the swamps of Flanders. From April 1915, bread, meat and sugar were rationed and from April 1917, as the German submarines sank more and more Allied merchantmen, all food was rationed and no concessions were made for locomotive firemen or coal miners upon whom the war effort depended – they got the same as office workers except that the latter had a larger helping of tea and sugar! Later on, an extra issue of cheese and biscuits was made to engine sheds so that men on long shifts, far away from home and starving hungry, could be offered some refreshment. Old-hand enginemen can still recall the Shed Foreman's well-worn question when they arrived in some distant engine shed: 'Had yer cheese and biscuits yet?'

The 'three Teds' in Crewe Junction box worked a treadmill of eight-hour shifts twenty days out of twenty-one – the most they could work in such a busy place. Other signalmen worked ten- or twelve-hour shifts according to the traffic they handled and the availability of relief but they were in the warm and dry and had definite hours; train guards and enginemen worked uncertain and frequently incredibly long hours, the men on freight work being the worst affected. A goods train from Worcester or Trowbridge would normally be twelve hours on the road to Southall and then nearly as long again on the last few miles to Acton or Paddington yards. Men marooned on a train in a goods loop or siding, waiting for a 'path', waiting for a space to be found for them in a goods yard, would eat all the food they had brought from home and then had to hope that they could buy food from a shop nearest the loop – always supposing the shopkeeper had food to sell 'off the ration'. Obviously many men went hungry and not surprisingly, to-wards the end of the war, influenza became a fatal disease of epidemic proportions in an overworked and underfed population. Railwaymen may have been physically fitter than other working people. In 1917 the Great Western gave their men the opportunity of extending their lineside allotments by offering new ground rent-free for the first year and at 3d a perch a year thereafter. Over 5000 men found the time and the energy to bring into cultivation 253 new lineside acres in addition to those already producing family food and for sale.

Enginemen found it hard to refuse to work ammunition or ambulance trains – they were carrying the fate of armies and for the most part they never forgot that – but their morale was not raised by hunger and exhaustion especially when they saw canteens set up by Church organisations, on railway stations, to dispense free food to soldiers and sailors and when the railway companies supplied Government-subsidised food through their refreshment rooms first to sailors and later to all servicemen. Jack Kinch told me that he was once away from home nine days on a sequence of ambulance and other war trains, sleeping where he could, begging the occasional sand-wich from the troops he was driving, getting a meal of 'off-the-ration' black-market spuds from a lodging-house lady whose husband bought a stock from food stolen out of the docks. Actually, Jack need not have been too jealous of the subsidised rations available to servicemen; for a shilling they got a pint of tea and two beef sandwiches, or a roll and lump of cheese or a small meat pie and a shilling was a day's pay. Soldiers travell-ing in small parties or alone carried a voucher, issued in barracks to the value of 6d, or a shilling to be used in station refreshment rooms but staff in these rooms also had instruc-tions to sell food, according to the 'menu' I have given above, to soldiers for cash. How could a man refuse to work an ambu-lance train? By late 1916 the wandering existence which the war situation demanded had become a terrible drain on engine-men's stamina and many began to refuse extra work – or even normal work – through sheer exhaustion. Enginemen's nerves would become taut through lack of sleep and if a driver and his fireman did not get on well together their life on the engine might well become intolerable as even small mannerisms might well assume grossly distorted proportions in men's tired minds. On 17 March 1917 Driver Smith and Fireman Davies of Hereford booked off at 4.25 p.m. on their home shed after fifteen hours on duty and each went to their beds to rest, ready for the next turn of duty at 5.50 a.m. next day. At 3 a.m. both men were woken by the shed call-boy carrying orders to report at once to the shed to relieve men who had been on long hours with an ambulance train. Both men refused, saying – and not without reason – that they were unwell. On 21 October Fireman Johnny Norton of Gloucester was woken at 1.30 a.m. and told to go direct to Cheltenham to relieve the fireman of an ambulance train.

'Who's my mate going to be?' he asked.

'Chapple,' replied the boy.

'Then I'm not coming,' said Norton and closed his bedroom window. Later, when called to account by Authority he told the Inspector that he had been stricken with a bad attack of rheumatism and was too ill to work. Authority let him off – as they did most staff. A man can take only so much punishment.

An additional hazard for enginemen and indeed for any man not in military uniform during the Great War was that of being assaulted in the street by a woman driven mad with grief and/or jingoism. At the end of a shift during which a man might have worked for fifteen hours on an ambulance train, he could be walking home and be attacked by some woman determined to attach to his person the white feather of cowardice.

To prevent this sort of thing happening the railway unions asked the War Office if their members could wear the 'War Service' lapel badge issued to munition workers and others engaged in 'reserved occupations' and not, therefore, liable to military service. In one of the most blimpish decisions of the war the request was refused on the grounds that railwaymen were not engaged in essential war work! Such nonsense only lowered railwaymen's morale.

On 10 August 1917, a Reading driver, Dick Davey, worked from his home shed to Plymouth in a continuous, 24-hour journey, rested there and at 4 a.m. on the 12th set out with a special for Acton. Over eight hours' travelling found him at Taunton, where he asked that relief be provided for him and his mate at Westbury and pressed slowly and doggedly on. Six hours later he steamed into Westbury, forty-four miles from Taunton to discover there was no relief whereupon he promptly backed the whole train, engine and all, into the yard and went home in the brake van of the 4.30 p.m. Weymouth to Clapham

Junction milk train, booking off in Reading after nineteen hours on the road and having been away from home for three days.

On 13 February 1917 Driver Chapman booked on at noon in Old Oak Common shed to work a special to Oxley (Wolverhampton) as far as Leamington. This was a 'cushy', 'single home' job, relief at Leamington and home 'on the cushions'. All went well, he and his mate got down the eighty-eight miles to Leamington in only eleven hours and, as they guessed, the signalman at the North box was ready with a message from 'Control' – 'would they care to take rest at Tyseley and then work another special south next day?' They agreed, travelled into Birmingham, booked off at midnight, slept in a lodging house and at 1 p.m. on the 14th set off with the south-bound special. It was a load of dynamite for Southampton docks. All afternoon and evening they stopped and started that train, crept through towns and villages, lurked in loops on the single-track line across the Berkshire downs. Midnight came and went. Chapman's wife gave up waiting for him back in Acton and went to bed. Still Chapman and his mate trundled on, over the Hampshire downs and finally into the docks at 4.40 a.m. on the 15th. Wearily they drove back 'light engine' to Eastleigh shed where the London & South Western Railway Foreman regaled them with cheese and biscuits, invited them to sample the delights of an Eastleigh lodging house and then to earn some more overtime on a special from Fareham to Oxford. Chapman was glad of the food but he had no money for more lodgings. The enginemen's lodging allowance had recently been increased but a man still had to pay the rent before he could claim it back and with no prospect of a hot meal or a bath he and his fireman said good-bye to the kind Foreman, left him their '43' class engine as a farewell gift and departed for Paddington on the first Southampton–Reading service that came along.

The year 1917 was very grim, with the civilian train service curtailed, the glossy Company liveries painted out as if in mourning for the dead and the cost of living 100 per cent higher than in 1914. A strike loomed and was headed off by a very small pay rise, the issue of that supplementary cheese and biscuit ration and the promise of the eight-hour day when the war was won. Most men struggled on. Some were conscripted into the army in spite of their importance to the war effort as railwaymen. Some actually volunteered to join the army just to get away from twelve- or fifteen-hour shifts – as Albert King, an old-hand Oxford driver and veteran of the Oxford & Bucks Light Infantry, told me with a wry smile.

SEVEN

Strikes and a Smoking-Out

When the Armistice was signed and the war brought to an end on 11 November 1918, the people of Britain went wild with joy – they had 'won the war' – and the very next day railway union leaders were knocking on the door of 10 Downing Street asking David Lloyd-George to honour his promise and grant the long-hoped-for eight-hour day. In much the same way as the Pied Piper of Hamelin was brushed aside by the Mayor and Corporation when he asked for payment ('what's dead can't come to life, I think,' said the Mayor) so the Prime Minister was not eager to comply now that the Emergency was over and the railways were no longer of supreme importance. While the Government demurred and the unions insisted, ordinary mortals tried to rebuild their shattered lives. Back to the Great Western from France came thousands of ex-staff members and hundreds of thousands of ex-soldiers who had never been railwaymen. Both these 'categories' had priority over those individuals who had held their railway jobs 'for the duration'.

Sid Tyler came to the Great Western in 1919 aged just over eighteen. He had joined the army at fourteen in September 1914 after putting his age up to nineteen, as he was quite tall. The Battle of the Somme he survived without a scratch although he was a front-line soldier, he was wounded in the Third Battle of Ypres, otherwise known evocatively as Passchendaele, and returned to his native town of Chippenham in 1918 to unemployment. Chippenham folk were intensely loyal, full of pride in their victory, their attitudes unchanged since 1913 – indeed, most people thought that the return of Peace

would bring a return of 1913. The returning soldiers knew
otherwise, they were changed men. Sid, once gentle and respectful of Authority, was now truculent and sick of orders. He
wanted work and he wanted to make his family understand the
squalor and the brutality of their victory – his recent experience. There was no work and no attempt at understanding;
instead there was a definite alienation between the group of
returned soliders and the rest of the town. The ex-servicemen
wanted to be the first to scan the 'jobs' columns of the local
paper and gathered early each morning outside a newsagent's
in a group which blocked the pavement. Chippenham folk
complained and a Constable was sent along to 'move them on'
but men who had endured life in flooded trenches and had
fought the greatest army in the world to a standstill and then
defeated it were in no mood to stand in the gutter to allow
civilians to pass nor to obey Constable Plod. Sid was fined 7s 6d
for obstructing the footpath.

At this point a girl he knew, one of a railway family, told him
that her ex-soldier brother had been offered and refused a
porter's job at Uffington, the original occupant not having
returned from the war. Sid applied and was granted the post
but for four years it had been occupied by one Ernie Gough who
had been taken on 'for the duration'. Needless to say Mr Gough
prepared to defend his job as best he could.

When Sid got off the up stopping train at Uffington Ernie
was there to meet him and without introducing himself too
precisely, offered to find him accommodation. Sid thought this
was very friendly and went along with Ernie into the railway
cutting and up its steep bank, into the village of Baulking to the
thatched, half-timbered cottage where Ernie lived with his
granny. The old lady was barely civil, the first meal was terrible
and the bed seemed damp, but as Sid knew less about Berkshire
than he did about Belgium he decided to stick it out in the hope
of an improvement. Next day he presented himself at the
station for his first day's work and discovered the full horror of
his situation when the porter from whom he was learning the

job said, 'You know whose job you're taking, don't you?' Sid could hardly face going back to the cottage but there was nowhere else and he tried to rationalise to calm his nerves – if it had not been him it would have been another ex-soldier who would have taken the job. Ernie Gough had known from the start that his employment was temporary, but no one then had guessed that the war would go on for four years. It was ridiculous to throw one man out to make room for another. Ernie waited on Sid at table, hovered around him solicitously, asking 'Do you think you'll like it here?' and Sid could hardly swallow his food.

After a mercifully short time a real vacancy arose at Wantage Road. Sid promptly applied for it, was transferred and Ernie Gough was reinstated at Uffington. Wantage Road was a very busy station with a staff of ten and the additional charm of Britain's first steam-hauled tram which ran along the roadside verges over the 2½ miles to the town, busily transferring goods and passengers, the freight going over the tramway in the main line companies' wagons. Before the Great War Wantage Road had enjoyed a slip carriage service off the rear of a down express and the tram engine, though forbidden to go on GWR metals, was used to pull the carriage off the main line into the sidings. Now the war was over the slip coach service was not reinstated but the kindly tramwaymen still used the tram engine for much GWR shunting so as to spare the shunting horse the effort. Sid had a willing, responsible attitude towards work, he got on well and soon conceived the ambition to be a Station Master. An application to the Bristol Divisional Superintendent produced an appointment for an interview with the great man who said, 'The best place you can go if you want to learn clerking is Seend. The Station Master there will sort you out.' 'Seend!' thought Sid. 'A glorified halt on the Devizes to Trowbridge line. What will I learn there?' The slightly sinister part of the Superintendent's pronouncement escaped him. Sid got out of the steam rail-car which served the station and asked the only man in sight 'Where's the Station Boss?' The man turned away without a word and went into an office. Sid followed, wondering what he had said wrong and discovered a very pretty girl busy with papers at a desk. He was just looking at her with increasing interest when the silent man said, icily, 'I am the Station Boss, as you put it, and this is my daughter whose job you will be taking.' The girl lifted her pretty head and gave Sid a poisonous glare which shattered his dreams of her and of the job. A few weeks at Seend, working in a 'sent to Coventry' conditions, smothered entirely his ambition to wear gold braid so that when a Class 6 signalman's job came up at Yarnbrook, near Westbury, he took it and thus began in mid-1920 a very happy period lasting forty-five years as a signalman.

Ben Davies worked from the moment he left school at thirteen in 1916. He could read, write and do sums, he was sensitive and even slightly nervous – irrelevant qualifications for a child of the Forest of Dean whose traditional fate was the low tunnels of the Forest coal mines. They were pitch dark, useless for reading so in the dark he sat on the rocky floor opening and closing a ventilation door as the men crawled by pulling sleds of coal with chains around their waists. For three years, twelve hours a day, Ben sat by his door until, in January 1919, he was old enough to apply for engine-cleaning work at the engine shed in Lydney. The Shed Foreman was suspicious of an urchin from the Forest – such people usually stuck to mining – and he had a number of questions to ask before he was satisfied with Ben's good character and would let him take the literacy and numeracy tests. These he passed but then the Foreman insisted that he go to the 'Panel' doctor in the town and get himself vaccinated for smallpox before he could start work. Ben was aghast. Doctors were an object of dread to a simple lad from the Forest and as for hypodermic syringes . . . He could not bring himself to face such an ordeal and walked home bitterly disappointed. However, after another two weeks down the mine, he went back to Lydney, had the injection and started as an engine cleaner. He could always recall the exact day. It was when David Lloyd-George finally honoured his promise and granted all railwaymen the eight-hour day: Monday 1 February 1919.

Though young Ben was more than thankful to be working in daylight the railway as a whole was uneasy. During the Great War railwaymen had put up with great hardship and now they wanted their inflation-rotted pay and their working conditions improved. The Associated Society of Locomotive Engineers and Firemen got standard rates of pay for all their members and the old system of pay rises through 'classification', where men had to wait until a vacancy occurred to move into a higher grade, was abolished in favour of a series of pay increases up to a maximum through 'steps' of a couple of years each. When the National Union of Railwaymen tried to obtain the same benefits for its men throughout Britain the negotiations failed, the footplate union joined with the NUR and the strike of 26 March 1919 was called.

Times had changed and the strike was popular even among Great Western men, much to the sorrow of the Company who put great trust in the public spirit of their men. Just for that moment, with the cost of living 120 per cent above that of 1913, the men had to put their own position and that of their dependents first. Not only did 94 per cent of the Goods and Traffic Department men strike and 65 per cent of footplatemen but 'regrettably', wrote the General Manager of the Great Western, Charles Aldington, '16 Station Masters, 304 Inspectors and 336 Foremen in Swindon works'. The Government was alarmed, the Army was placed on alert to assist the civil power and Lloyd-George wrote to Aldington, 'No measures have been omitted which might have prevented this strike and I am convinced there is something more behind it than mere wages and conditions. Please instruct your Chief Officers to do everything in their power to carry on and break the strike.'

There were plenty of volunteers from salaried staff, GWR pensioners and enthusiasts, all eager to lay their hands on a shovel or a signal lever or even just to do portering and muck out cattle trucks. Sir Edward Nichols who had worked a

seven-year apprenticeship in Swindon factory drove engines
and an equerry of King George came to Paddington as a porter.
The trains that were run into Paddington gave the place a
somewhat Indian atmosphere in as much as they were so
packed with passengers that people were riding on the engines'
front buffer beams. The '517' class tank-engine of the Marlow
branch train – the 'Marlow Donkey' – was manned by enthusiasts but one evening, while they were at supper, some striking
enginemen crept up, threw out the engine's fire and then
opened the 'blow-down cock' to drain the boiler. The roar of
escaping steam brought the volunteers running from their hut
and covered the wily strikers' rapid exit in a perfect fog of
vapour.

The Great Western's goods and parcel delivery service was
almost entirely horse-drawn and several volunteer-driven
drays were immobilised by strikers who waylaid them, like
highwaymen of old, and stole the bit from between the horses'
teeth. Animals were quite a problem for the Company, not so
much in the towns and cities where people and societies such as
the RSPCA went into railway stables and sidings to feed and
water horses and cattle, but in the country where trains of cattle
were abandoned in goods loops or station yards. At Fishguard
where there was a constant stampede of Irish cattle from boat
to trains, hundreds of cattle had to be found temporary grazing
in fields for miles around and people had to be found to drive
them to their refuges and to take them water. With 94 per cent
of the workforce on strike all this took a lot of organising and led
to some bitter scenes, some rather more angry than thoughtful.
At Swindon some strikers painted black the front door of a man
whom they thought was still working – they had the right man
but the wrong door and spent the rest of the strike cleaning the
door and re-painting it. At Knighton Crossing, twelve miles
east of Swindon, one signalman remained at work until he
turned up and found that the instruments had been smashed.
The 9.40 a.m. up from Bristol, hauled by a 'Saint' class express
engine, ran into a large pile of sleepers on the track between

Wootton Bassett and Swindon and scattered them in all directions doing little harm but soon afterwards the enginemen spotted the little 'Swindon Motor', a steam-engined rail-car heading down line. By dint of much waving and whistling they managed to stop it, otherwise there may well have been a derailment. The Swindon District Inspector took a 'light engine' to the site, carrying an armed guard and together they cleared the line.

The strike ended on 5 October 1919 with a victory for the railwaymen in that they gained a minimum wage of 52 shillings a week so long as the cost of living was 110 per cent above that of 1913 but they had also allowed onto the scene the first of the road lorries and their ex-army drivers. The vehicles were primitive and so were the roads but they had proved their worth. As the Great Western was faced with trebly increased costs over 1913 and was forced to increase fares and cartage rates there was an embryo competitor waiting to pick up the traffic. Rising costs were only part of a worrying situation for the Directors and Chief Officers of the Great Western in that turbulent, post-war period. The Bolshevik Revolution had provided everyone with a very bloody example of how one form of Socialism might arrive, an example which terrified or elated according to one's point of view. The status quo of 1913 had certainly not returned, indeed, to many people it seemed as if the world was going mad. There were loud noises from some quarters in favour of nationalising the railways as a step towards Utopia and one Member of Parliament actually went so far as to assert that money taken at railway booking offices was in fact Public Property. The Great Western Directors were alarmed and any action by Great Western staff that even remotely resembled indiscipline was jumped on. In January 1920 this note was sent from the General Manager to the Divisional Superintendent at Bristol: 'Laxity is occurring whereby the men book-on late and take more than their hour for dinner. They must be properly supervised and stopped.' Outright mutiny left the General Manager rather more bemused, less decisive. In May 1920 there was a strike at the brickworks of Messrs Board Ltd, whose kilns were situated by the lineside at Dunball, south of Highbridge. Road access to them was over a level-crossing controlled from Dunball box and rail access was also controlled from the box. Board's tried to keep their works going but Signalmen Harker and Clark refused to open the gates to road lorries and refused to pull the points to allow the local 'Fly' into the sidings. It was all quite impromptu, out of genuine sympathy for the brickworks men, and the General Manager at Paddington was at a loss to know how to deal with this unprecedented event. He wrote a puzzled note to the Bristol Superintendent, 'The action of Great Western men in behaving thus is extraordinary and, strictly speaking, I presume they ought to be suspended for refusing to carry out legitimate work for which they are employed and paid. However, before any action is taken I should be glad to hear from you.' Bristol sent the District Inspector down to Dunball to have a word with the men; they agreed to work normally pending a decision from the NUR; everyone was then 'off the hook' and the matter rested.

The Great Western was in a relatively chaotic state during 1920 as a result of a shortage of motive power – engines were in works being repaired after the neglect of the war period – and simply sheer volume of traffic. For instance, at 11 a.m. 5 February 1920 there were 'dead' (i.e. locomotiveless) trains in goods loops at Hay Lane, Hullavington, Bathampton, Twerton, Keynsham and Fox's Wood. In Bristol East Depot marshalling yard there were 500 loaded wagons for the west of England, 200 for the west of Wales and 300 for destinations east of Bristol all stuck for lack of power. Thus the sorting sidings were blocked against incoming trains which then languished in outlying goods loops until their drivers decided they had had enough, 'cut the engine off' and went home to shed.

Throughout 1920, and indeed throughout the decade, demand for transport increased and the Great Western never turned traffic away. In fact, carters on their drays, station

masters at country stations and Divisional Goods Managers
went out canvassing for more. Quite apart from keeping the
trucks of the regular goods trains filled, the railway filled
innumerable specials carrying every conceivable traffic from
Territorial Army units to their Annual Camp on Salisbury
Plain to Sunday School children on their annual treat to
Weymouth or Weston-super-Mare. Perhaps there was a race
meeting at Newmarket – a 'light engine' with brake-composite
coach attached would leave Swindon for Marlborough via the
old M&SW and return, picking up horse boxes at all stations
over the Wiltshire Downs and along the Vale of the White
Horse before galloping away at passenger train speed for Acton
and the North London line to hand over to the Great Eastern
Railway. Monthly cattle fairs at Trowbridge or Malmesbury,
Cleobury Mortimer or Frome required extra staff to be posted
to those towns to help with the extra work and trains of cattle
wagons. The seasonal landings of daffodils and new potatoes at
Weymouth and Penzance provided six weeks' heavy work for
the extra engines and men drafted in from other depots; there
were the Cheddar Valley strawberry trains, the Vale of
Evesham plum trains, Christmas parcel post trains, Tidworth
Tattoo specials and, every winter Saturday, football specials
three or four at a time from Bristol to Cardiff or Birmingham to
Plymouth. At Easter, Christmas and throughout the long
summer holiday period, June to September, and at the Bank
Holiday week-ends when the normal time-tables had to be
suspended to provide engines and coaches for the vast crowds,
trains ran in three, four or even five parts – whilst at main
depots along the line 'emergency' trains each comprising
twelve coaches and engine stood ready to mop up surplus
passengers.

On 11 November 1920 all this mighty roar of traffic came to a
sudden and complete standstill such as was never achieved by
any strike. Earlier, the General Manager had written to all
Divisional Superintendents, 'It is the intention of His Majesty's
Government that there should be a complete cessation of all

normal activity for two minutes at 11 a.m. on Thursday 11 November. Trains due to depart at 11 a.m. must be detained for two minutes and running trains must be stopped as near as possible at that time but not on steep gradients, high bridges, viaducts or in tunnels.' This request was carried out on the Great Western to the letter. At 10.59 a.m. that day, Bristol Temple Meads station was its usual, noisy self, crowds milling, trolleys rattling along loaded with churns or parcels but, at eleven o'clock, without any overt signal, the entire place became as still and silent as if it had been deserted. Nothing stirred, not an engine hissed and all men stood, bareheaded, for two minutes under the cavernous, dark roof, in silent homage and remembrance of their friends and relations killed in the Great War.

Against this grim background – the nation in a state of shock after the late and totally horrific war, rising costs and industrial unrest as men tried to earn a crust – the Great Western tried to cope with its responsibilities. A pre-war passenger train service complete with slip coaches and restaurant cars was reinstated from 5 May 1919 and in October 1921 pre-war speeds were written into the time-tables. By this time the Great Western was once more its own master for the Railways Act, repealing wartime Government control, was passed on 19 August 1921, and in this same Act 120 railway companies were grouped into 'The Big Four': London, Midland & Scottish; London & North Eastern; Southern; and Great Western Railways. The Great Western was so big that it could not be amalgamated with any other concern so it was given a few small lines like the Cambrian and the Midland & South Western Junction and allowed to keep its majestic old title.

The magnificent train service for passengers off transatlantic liners at Fishguard was never re-established, neither were the highly enterprising day trips to Killarney but the Plymouth Ocean Mails continued and, of course, the 'Cornish Riviera', the longest non-stop run in the world – 10.30 a.m. from Paddington to Plymouth, 225¾ miles in 247 minutes at an overall average of 54.8 mph. This, and the return working, was a very serious business, especially for the firemen upon whose physical fitness the whole legend depended but on 9 July 1923 the Great Western introduced a timing for a show train which instantly became a kind of game for skilled, top link, engine crews. The 2.30 p.m. from Cheltenham to Paddington was retimed to run non-stop from Swindon to Paddington, 77¼ miles in seventy-five minutes with a load of nine coaches. Swindon men had the job and on the first day Driver Hopkins and Fireman Bailey, with Chief Inspector Flewellyn on the footplate, took 2915 *Saint Bartholomew* up to London in seventy-two minutes. Brunel's road was, at Swindon, level with the top of St Paul's Cathedral in London so the gentle, downhill inclination without a sharp curve in the entire distance made an ideal race-track and, given the incentive, drivers and firemen were keen to have a go for a spectacular and relatively easy sprint – just for the glory. Swindon men and others were soon knocking ten minutes off the schedule, any train that was a Swindon–Paddington non-stop was a candidate and even those with fourteen coaches on were known to keep to the seventy-five-minute schedule.

It was very sad that, with so much goodwill and enthusiasm, there should still have been the need for strikes but on 24 January 1924 impending wage cuts for drivers brought about as ASLEF strike which the NUR men were ordered, by their union, not to support. The strike lasted a few days and was successful in drastically reducing the amount of proposed cuts. On 6 August 1924, Mr R.H. Nicholls, Superintendent of the Line, was in Bristol entertaining some of his Officers to lunch in the saloon carriage in which he rode when travelling about the railway. The saloon had been specially parked on one of the Middle Sidings under the Brunellian Baronial roof of the Old Station at Temple Meads, a relatively quiet corner of a very busy place. The Officers were steadily tucking into a lordly menu such as no other railway had provided for their executives since 1913. At 1.21 p.m., just as they were having their third glass and were beginning to stretch their legs out a bit, a little 0–4–2 tank engine '517' class 1463 came silently along-side, against the buffers a track or two removed from the saloon. It had just worked in off the 11.22 a.m. from Swindon stopping train, standing in for a failed steam rail-motor. Its next job was the 3.40 p.m. to Bath and in the meantime the driver expected to propel the engine and coach to shed. Time passed, signals were not lowered, the driver looked across at the Officers noshing away off porcelain and damask and the temptation was too great to resist. 'Put a bit round, son,' he commanded. His young mate looked surprised but the old driver nodded over towards the saloon. The fireman understood, grinned broadly and put some big lumps of coal on the fire. Presently green smoke oozed out of the chimney and a gentle draught carried it across to the Officers' saloon. It was a grand joke, a little smoking would do them no harm and after the length of time 1463 had been standing it would not be very long before the engine was moved – or so thought the driver – but he had been forgotten and it was not until 3.5 p.m. that his engine was moved on and only then at the irate orders of Nicholls himself when his saloon was full of green smoke. The Station Foreman, Mr Driscoll, had to 'carry the can' – him and the driver. The tale went the rounds and the chuckles it raised far outweighed the bother of the tickings-off that were meted out.

On 4 May 1926 a nationwide strike was called in support of the miners whose wages were to be reduced. By no means the entire country supported this General Strike but most railway-men came out along with other men in heavy industry. When the last railwayman finally went back to work on the 14th nothing had been achieved and road transport had got its foot firmly in the door as a national carrier. The strike did not stop all Great Western trains. Driver Edley Ponting, based at Fairford, was one of two men who kept the Fairford branch running. On the Wallingford branch, a consulting engineer from Raynes Park, Mr J.H. Clarke, drove the branch engine which was fired by a GWR pensioner, Mr Pearce. On the main line, right from the start, some trains ran, milk for London being given priority.

Volunteers there were in plenty to work the trains, the signal boxes and the stations but as Albert King, who was on the Strike Action Committee, said wryly – 'there were no volunteers to go down the mines.' Oxford's busmen worked throughout the strike and at a special meeting called to try to persuade them to join the railwaymen, Albert King and Harry Keen, who was now at Oxford from Slough, were shouted down with cries from the road transport men of 'Why should we go on strike?' The South Midland Motor Bus Company provided a bus service to replace the train on the Abingdon to Oxford service and also between Oxford and London. The roads were like country lanes for most of the way and the buses had solid tyres but the public saw that there was an alternative to trains and one that did not seem to be continuously on strike. William Morris's factory at Morris Cowley did not go on strike and Morris (later Lord Nuffield) took whole-page advertisements in the *Oxford Times* to drive home the point. 'Morris trucks and cars will help you carry on through the strike' and they did too. Oxford undergraduates went in Morris cars to Hull and Bristol docks where they unloaded ships and got into fights with 'rowdies' and they worked on the Oxford stations. A General Strike could be the prelude to Red Revolution – coal was rationed and milk went up in price to a penny a pint. Large numbers of people rallied round and by 6 May several trains a day were running between Paddington and Worcester and Birmingham via Oxford.

The strike finally collapsed for the railways on 14 May. Soon afterwards a letter arrived on the Oxford Station Master's desk, from the Lord Mayor of Oxford, inviting half a dozen 'loyal' railwaymen round to the Town Hall for a rewarding tea. The Station Master merely handed the letter to Harry Keen who was the local union representative and Harry picked himself and five strikers, including Albert King, to go and have tea with the Mayor. A really slap-up affair it was, too, with all the city's silver plate including the Mace on view. The six of them, along with a large party of busmen – who loyally did not let on to the Mayor who the railwaymen really were – were given a guided tour and an official 'thank-you' from the assembled dignitaries for having done their best to keep the Red Terror at bay. At the age of ninety, Harry Keen could still chuckle at the memory.

EIGHT

Tricksters of the Twenties

Great Western staff were acknowledged by the GWR Police Department to be a very honest body of men. Thefts of all kinds were a constant problem on the railway but in a check made at Banbury on passengers' luggage in transit between the GWR and LNER it was proved that most theft took place on LNER metals. Where tens of thousands of men are employed there are bound to be a few who succumb to temptation. In 1927 at Tonypandy, for example, a porter, whose brother-in-law's garden bordered the railway line close to the station, was caught handing interesting-looking parcels over the garden fence. A Worcester passenger train guard carried a bunch of skeleton keys with which he unlocked suitcases and removed any small, saleable items. His 'fence' was a prostitute in Birmingham. In Cornwall, a GWR bus inspector and three conductors were operating a black market in return halves of tickets, not 'cancelling' them but selling them again. Marked tickets and careful surveillance brought about the men's downfall. They were taken before the magistrates but the Bench took such a lenient view of the matter that the GWR Police Inspector, Mr Pine, was obliged to administer to the Magistrates 'a dignified reproof in unmistakable language' and *ordered* them – under the powers conferred on the police by the Vexatious Indictments Act – to commit the accused for trial at the Quarter Sessions. This happened in 1928 and was the very first time that the GWR Police Department had taken advantage of these powers. The Inspector of Buses got six months and his accomplices four months each.

Return halves, being valid for three months, were easily re-used by silly Travelling Ticket Collectors (TTC) on trains and a constant watch was kept to try to stamp out this particular black market. The wife of a GWR policeman was used to hand a secretly marked ticket to a TTC on a Swansea to Paddington express in 1928. At Paddington the man's ticket bundle was checked when he handed it in and the marked ticket was missing. He was searched and the ticket together with two more were found interspersed within the leaves of his excess fare ticket pad. In spite of having twenty-one years' service and the fact that in 1927 another Swansea TTC had been dismissed for the same offence, this daft man had 'tried it on' – and he paid the price by losing his job.

Ticket frauds were by no means the preserve of railway staff. In 1928, blank card tickets (those on which the destination was hand-written) were turning up bearing a printed type-face not in accordance with GWR specification. The Chief Accountant's Office sent the tickets to the GWR Police Department where they were microscopically examined but no trace of any mutilation could be seen so they were sent to the GWR chemist in Swindon works to see if he could tell whether the original writing had been removed and, if so, by what means. The chemist reported that a chemical had been used to erase the lettering and new print and writing had then been superimposed. The chances of catching the culprit seemed remote but the GWR Police Department gave it some thought and cast their net into the area from where most GWR blank card tickets were issued – the twenty-five London branches of Thomas Cook, travel agents. The forger used 1st class blank cards because their face value was greater when it came to re-sale but he would want to buy his raw material cheaply so he would use a ticket costing less than, say, 5 shillings. Cook's were asked to provide each evening a list of all 1st class GWR blank cards sold that day for 5 shillings or less. On 26 September 1928 the Police Department were told that 1st class blank card No 427, Paddington to Southall, had been issued at the Hotel Russell on the 25th.

The face of the ticket was even then, the police knew, being re-processed so they warned station masters at principal stations west of Bristol and north of Banbury to instruct their ticket-collecting staff to be on the look-out for 1st class blank card No 427 and to keep the bearer under observation when they found him or her. At midday on the 27th the sharp-eyed ticket collector on the gate at Highbridge was handed the 'hot' ticket – now marked Newquay–Paddington – by a man heading off the up fast for the Somerset & Dorset Railway station and a train to Templecombe. The Highbridge station master invited the man to enter his office and to remain there until a constable could come down from Bristol. This he agreed to do and was held until 2.40 a.m. on the 28th when he and the constable went up to Paddington on the up TPO. He was interrogated for several hours before he admitted using 'Sodae Chlorinat' to expunge the original lettering and admitted a conspiracy between him (an engineer) and others to forge tickets. No amount of questioning would make him reveal his associates' names, except to say they were all of professional standing and he went down, alone, from the dock of the Old Bailey to do four months in gaol for forgery.

Another form of passenger trickster was the card-sharp. Though he was probably more common in the nineteenth century he still haunted the trains, especially the excursions to the races, in the 1920s and 1930s. Their most effective trick was the oldest in the book – there was always some 'gull' about waiting to be plucked. The card-sharp worked with an accomplice who played the part of the disinterested stranger. He would be invited to say where, in three cards, the Ace lay, having watched them being moved from place to place in the 'fan'. He would win more often than he lost, the 'gull' – or 'gulls' – would be consumed with interest; he was, after all, a bit of a gambler, off to the races. The sharp watched him carefully and when he had him hooked offered him the chance to win some money. Few people had the courage to complain when they fell victim to the age-old 'three-card trick' but one man did when he got off a Paddington–Windsor race special. The two sharps were arrested and the silly 'gull' got his money back. He had lost no less than £65 in twenty minutes.

The Banks and the GPO sent thousands of pounds in used notes by rail in ordinary mail sacks which were tossed into the guard's van along with all the other sacks and parcels. Anonymity was a defence against theft until some crook gained 'inside' knowledge when the theft became merely a matter of throwing the bag out of a window to an accomplice waiting on the lineside. For years the GWR Chief Constable urged proper precautions but he was ignored. On 4 December 1928 the 7.6 p.m. train from Gloucester terminated at Swindon, its passengers and freight being transferred across the platform to the waiting 6.50 p.m. Weston-super-Mare to Paddington express. Among the bags transferred was one containing £4000 comprising used £5 and £10 notes. While the work was going on a well-dressed young woman came to the guard of the 6.50 Weston and asked him to come with her to find an empty compartment because, she said, she had bronchitis and did not want to disturb other passengers with her racking cough. The guard found her such a compartment three coaches forward from his van, the lady climbed in and asked if he would be so kind as to visit her during the journey to make sure she was all right. The guard found this quite an agreeable chore and readily said 'Yes'. The train left at 8.50 p.m. and as they were passing Didcot he thought he would go forward and have a chat to the personable woman. She kept him for five minutes with a long and rather boring story about how she had come down to Swindon to find her estranged husband but had not found him and was going home. Very boring. The guard took his leave and went back to his van. When it was unloaded at Paddington the sack of money had disappeared and so had the young woman who had kept him out of his van for five minutes.

Wagons standing in sidings were sitting targets, especially in the mining areas of South Wales where wagon raids were a nightly occurrence in the 1920s. The police were hopelessly outnumbered but made an effort to catch a few by concentrating their efforts. Two policemen rode in the guard's van of a freight train from Merthyr to Aberdare. When it arrived in Quakers' Yard sidings the guard went to the front to uncouple some trucks and as he went between the wagons three men came out from a hut and began to rifle the wagon next to the van where the police were hiding. The van door was narrow so the police could not make a rapid exit. They feared the thieves would escape if they made a sudden sally but then the situation resolved itself because the man who was obviously the ringleader decided to board the van. He came through the door with a policeman flattened against the wall on each side and was nabbed. He put up a stiff fight but he was overpowered. He was an ex-convict who had moved down from London to take advantage of the situation in South Wales and had a lorry to take the swag back to London. The Great Western did not pursue the reason for the 'master-mind' wanting to go back to the guard's van though it could easily have been the case that he and the guard were in collusion. Wagons arriving at Neath from Birkenhead and the Midlands were being raided en route and the chance discovery of wrappers off goods in a wood near Little Mill Junction alerted the police who staked out the wood and the sidings at Little Mill. Early one Sunday morning a father and son team arrived, broke into some wagons and removed a big bale of blankets. The police moved in, there was a fierce fight and the miscreants were overpowered. The father got six months and the son was bound over to keep the peace. The police often spent night after night, patiently waiting for thieves to turn up and then had to resort to fists and truncheons in some quite desperate affrays. So used were they to night-time robbery that wagons between Shrewsbury and Bridgnorth were raided with impunity for weeks before the police decided the offences must have been taking place when they were not on watch – during daylight. A spot check on Coalport Sidings caught two signalmen red-handed, raiding trucks.

The resultant swag from these raids could still lead to the

arrest of the culprit. Bales of trousers made at a factory in Blower's Green near Dudley were going missing during rail transit and the culprit took two pairs into a clothing outfitters in Worcester for alteration. Now it so happened that this shop was the sole agent for that factory's clothing in Worcester yet the man who brought the garments in said he had purchased them at another shop in the town. The shopkeeper promptly wrote an irate letter to the manufacturer complaining that they had broken the agency agreement and the factory replied demanding proof. The trousers were duly sent along and were recognised as belonging to the batches which had gone missing. When the man came back for his altered trousers he found the GWR police waiting for him.

Luggage thieves were a constant nuisance to passengers and cost the Great Western dearly in claims. It was not often that such thieves gave prior notice of their activities but one day in 1927, following the theft of a suitcase from the cloakroom at Birkenhead station, the station master there received the following note:

> 'I'm just off down Bristol way with the dressing case from your cloakroom. I've played them up at Liverpool, Chester, Wigan, Bolton and Preston so I think it's time to clear. I'll be in Bristol by the time you get this,
>
> Yours, ever so sorry.

The man kept his word, everyone was on the look-out for him and he was caught on Bath station. Poor chap, he was fifty-seven years old and in his time he had served twenty years in gaol. Maybe he was getting tired and wanted to go inside as a rest from wandering the land. He went down for five years.

The Great Western Railway's policemen obviously put a great deal of patient effort – even a little of their own blood – into trying to control railway crime. The Chief Constable stated officially in 1927 that the 3180 prosecutions of that year would have been quite impossible to obtain without 'the unswerving loyalty and co-operation of my entire staff'. In the same report he also stated, 'In deference to your [the Board of Directors] general appeal for greater economy I have already succeeded in effecting substantial savings by reducing personnel (as shown) thus saving £15,000 per annum.

		Present Strength
Inspectors	4	29
Sergeants	6	42
Detectives	6	32
Constables	62	265

Badminton station was opened in July 1903 at the lonely Cotswold summit of the Great Western's new, short route to Bristol and South Wales. The tracks passed through the beautiful, Gloucestershire estates of the Duke of Beaufort who, as part of his price for allowing the new line across his land, retained the right to stop express trains to and from London – though such an aristocratic line as the Great Western would not have been so churlish, in any case, as to refuse a Duke the 'out of course' use of the odd, long-distance express. The right was written into the Deed of Conveyance; the Ducal arms, emblazoned on tablets of stone, were embedded in the walls of the station's buildings. To cater for the Duke the 7.50 a.m. Pembroke Dock to Paddington and the 1.18 p.m. Paddington to Swansea called daily in 1929 while the 12.45 p.m. Neyland and the 3.55 p.m. Paddington were booked to call 'if required'. The station yard was frequently a bustle of activity as milk and farm produce was loaded from horse-drawn wagons while the Ducal Daimler waited to pick up some privileged visitor to Badminton House. During the winter months the yard was often full of hounds and horses as the Beaufort Hunt was loaded into a special train to carry it to the site of the Meet.

Sid Tyler moved from Yarnbrook to Badminton in 1927 where he sometimes played host to the Royal children, brought down to the station to watch the trains by their nurse. The aristocracy of England used the box as a waiting room and with a cheerful man like Sid presiding that was perfectly understandable.

Just before Christmas 1927 the 3.55 p.m. Paddington made a special stop to set down passengers for Badminton House and a very stately lady, accompanied by a gentleman and their personal servants, descended onto the platform. There followed an altercation between the gentleman and the guard which caused some delay in the train's departure but at last the 'Star' class engine whistled-up, barked away into the night and Sid put it 'on line' to Chipping Sodbury. The lady was the Dowager Duchess of Cambridge, King George's sister; the gentleman was one Algy Stanley, brother to Lord Derby. They were well wrapped-up against the cold, and after settling into the Daimler were driven away. The only really odd thing about the entire scene was that they had no luggage and people like them usually had a four-wheel barrowful. They were driven away with the most ruffled feelings, their Christmas was entirely ruined and shortly afterwards the following letter arrived at Paddington from the Duchess, addressed to the Chairman of the Great Western Board of Directors, Victor, Viscount Churchill:

Dear Victor,

Please forgive me worrying you in this way. There is a young man I am very much interested in – I sent you a paper with his description. Could you please help to get him on? He is a most excellent young man aged 24. I should be so glad if you could.

I have a big complaint to make against your railway and not least against one of the guards on the 3.55 p.m. train from Paddington to Cardiff. I went down to Badminton on 22nd December and stopped the train there. There were 400 too many people on the train and when we (I went down with Algy Stanley) tried to get our luggage the people had taken it out of the van and were sitting on it through all the corridors of the train. We could not turn all those people out and they would not get off our boxes. All my Christmas presents were inside. The train guard would not wait and our luggage was taken all the way to Cardiff. The point of this story is that I think the guard should lock his van and not let anyone remove its contents. Also the brakes on the train would not work which seems to me rather dangerous and Algy said he was going to write to you about it. It was very badly done and another train would have been better than all that mass of people in one train. The guard said the brakes wouldn't work because of the weight of people in the train. I thought you ought to know. How are you?

Yours sincerely,
Marchioness of Cambridge

Which goes to show that working the world's most aristocratic railway had its drawbacks – such as having to deal with an irate Dowager Duchess. Churchill made inquiries with the General Manager, Felix Pole, a man who had risen to that position from telegraph office messenger at Reading. This was Pole's reply:

Dear Sir,

The 3.55 was exceptional. In addition to this we ran a 3.45 and a 4.5 to South Wales. We thought, from previous experience, that this would lift the traffic but we were overwhelmed by an unexpectedly large number of ex-Welsh miners, who had found work in London, returning home to South Wales for Christmas. They arrived without warning and the confusion at No 2 booking office and at the barriers was immense. They stormed the train which quickly had to be strengthened (with extra coaches) and it eventually left with 15 on carrying 900 people. The 3.45 had already taken 1500 and the 4.5 took 1100 and still it was necessary to get another train together, leaving at 5 p.m. with 600 people. A total of 4100 travelled to South Wales between 3.45 and 5 p.m. The overspill from the 3.45 into the 4.5 was so great that the van was packed with passengers. The over-carrying of the Marchioness' luggage is much to be regretted but there is no doubt that the guard was powerless to help in the matter.

With regard to the brakes. The train was stopped at Old Oak Common West after Ladbroke Grove sent 7 bells ('Stop & Examine') for sparks off the rear wheels. Nothing found. 7 bells stopped the train at Ealing and Hayes. Nothing found. But at Hayes the examiner slacked off the brake-shoes. It was stopped again and Waltham and Milton. Nothing found. It then went on without further delay.

It sounded like a perfectly frightful journey for the jam-packed passengers. It is also pleasantly reassuring to hear the General Manager defending the guard of the 3.55 against the Marchioness. This was Churchill's reply to her:

> I have had your complaint investigated and find that our arrangements were utterly upset by large numbers of ex-Welsh miners and their families, who had drifted to London in search of work, suddenly descending on Paddington to return home for Christmas. The advertised arrangements were based on previous experience and would have been sufficient but for these unforeseen circumstances. I can only express my deep regret that you should have had such a disagreeable journey. As to the brakes there was nothing wrong with them and the delays were due to some adjustments that were needed. With regard to your young man Howarth, I am sorry to say that we have been lately reducing our staff owing to the bad times and the prospects of our needing men in the S&T Department are remote. I have asked my people to keep his name before them.
>
> Victor Churchill

Westwards from Badminton the line fell at 1 in 300 for many miles, through the 4444-yds-long Chipping Sodbury tunnel, falling all the way until it was 30 ft below the river Severn in a tunnel 4½ miles long, at the west end of which lay the big engine shed and vast sidings of Severn Tunnel Junction. Ben Davies came to the Severn Tunnel about 1930 after working at Lydney, Neath and Penzance and spent much of his time on the Severn Tunnel bankers. These were usually the powerful '31' class 2–6–2 tanks introduced by G.J. Churchward in 1906, used to assist any train with an overload for the long climb at 1 in 100 from tunnel bottom up to Pilning or even to Stoke Gifford on the English side. The load of every up train was 'wired' to

Severn Tunnel Middle box so that those which were over-loaded for the tunnel were known about in advance. Such was the demand for banking power that five bankers were employed during the day and four at night, eight of them working for sixteen hours and one for eight – the men working an eight-hour day.

Every train which took a bank engine took on its rear a special, 25-ton, 'Severn Tunnel' brake-van, 5 tons heavier than normal, running on a six-wheel chassis. Each brake-van was totally enclosed to give the guard some protection from the heavy, sulphurous exhaust from two engines working hard within the 'Big Hole' as the tunnel was called. The 25-ton van was pushed up onto a ramp with others by the banker which then went to take its place on the reserved siding. An Inspector working with the signalman in Severn Tunnel Middle box warned the enginemen, 'You'll be banking the Aberdare in ten minutes,' and Ben would look to his fire. When the train arrived the banker 'dropped on top' of the train engine (and was therefore strictly speaking a 'Pilot' engine) and the banker alone pulled the train forward. The 25-ton brake-van could thus be gravitated down off the ramp to couple-up behind the ordinary brake-van. If the second van stopped short, the yard staff sounded a klaxon so that the bank engine crew would know to set back. When they finally got the road, the banker alone hauled the train forwards towards the tunnel and was frequently routed into the goods loop to await a path through that notorious bottleneck. The line fell at 1 in 90 so the guards and firemen used their hand-brakes to control the train's progress and the driver used the vacuum-brake simply to make the final stop if even that was necessary. There was only one up line through the tunnel, traffic was heavy and trains had to take a definite, minimum time on their passage through. Express trains were supposed to be six minutes from Tunnel East to Tunnel West boxes or vice-versa and the heavy, unbraked freights were supposed to take a minimum of fifteen minutes for the 4½ miles. Eventually there would be a 'path' for Ben's heavy coal train; the loop points came over; the loop exit signal was lowered; the brakes released; and the train would roll forward, down the slope from Severn Tunnel West box, through the slimy, wet, rock cutting into the smoking mouth of the 'Big Hole'. The three-link chain couplings of coal trucks in those days were appreciably longer than those of the 1950s, so a sixty-wagon train had a lot of slack chain to pick up. Gravity took the train for a mile with the guards' brakes dragging back to stop the wagons running up against each other, then the banker began to pull, running on slightly faster to draw out all couplings taut, gently so that when the train reached the twelve chains of level track in the bottom of the tunnel the train would be strung out, couplings taut ready for the abrupt change of gradient as the line climbed out of the tunnel on a 1 in 100 gradient. Controlled in this manner there were no slack chains which might otherwise be tugged taut so sharply as to break them – and if the guards were left behind in that smoke-thick hell-hole they might have been asphyxiated.

All this skilled handling of hundreds of lumbering tons was, it must be remembered, done in total darkness made worse by smoke so thick that sometimes Ben could not see his mate across the cab and there were times when they both had to lie down on the footplate to breathe the slightly less polluted air nearer the rails. Going uphill the train engine came into the fight and both machines blazed away with their firemen shovelling fresh coal into the fire and maybe they would pass another coal train working to draw out couplings on the down line. No wonder the air was 'as thick as a bag' and the lights provided at tunnel bottom to mark the start of the level track and the start of the climb out were invisible. The tunnel banker men used their own indicator to show when the gradient changed. They opened the top doors to the coal bunker and while they were going downhill the doors hung forward, into the cab but when the gradient changed they swung back against the bunker. It was an infallible guide so long as plenty of oil was poured on the hinges. At the change of gradient, the bank engine would already be working in 30 per cent cut-off and full regulator, the banker's driver would blow crows on his whistle for the train engine's effort and, deep under the Severn estuary, both engines would set-to, hammer and tongs in a deafening, choking roar.

The hardest job for the Severn Tunnel enginemen was the 3.50 p.m. Milford Haven 'Trawl Fish', 'double home' to Paddington 123 miles away, calling at Swindon and Reading to pick up empty coaches. It was a fully vacuum-braked, 'C' headcode goods train hauled by a big engine and alongside its entry in the Working Time-Table was the warning to signalmen, 'Other goods trains to be kept clear'. The 'Trawl Fish' was one of *the* 'crack' freight trains of the Great Western. 'Double home' meant lodging away overnight. Some men hated this, others quite enjoyed the break from their wife. Some took a positively nautical attitude to the practice and had a lady friend at the other end of the line – or so legend has it. Most men just accepted 'double homing' as part of the job. It all depended on what kind of lodgings a man could find. Some houses were very clean, run by an engine driver's widow perhaps, who never overcrowded her accommodation, where everything was spotlessly clean and there was plenty to eat; such a 'lodge' probably catered for a very limited and regular clientele who treated the place carefully as if it was their own. Other places were more akin to the lower class of doss-house.

Ben Davies had not done a 'double home' turn when he was called on to fire a 'Saint' on the 'Trawl Fish' at 10 p.m. after the regular fireman had gone sick. The driver was a cantankerous old cuss whose temper was not improved by the arrival on his footplate of a stranger from a lower link and Ben knew before they started that he was in for a rough trip. The engine steamed well which was fortunate for the train pulled like lead on the twenty uphill miles to Badminton and was not a great deal better on the downhill stretches. Ben stood before the firehole and kept on shovelling until, more dead than alive, they arrived at Paddington at 1.30 a.m. They backed gently down the engine line to Old Oak Common shed, Ben's eyes closing every now and then involuntarily. The engine was left with the firedroppers – Ben sincerely thanked the Great Western Directors for not allowing their enginemen to 'dispose' of engines at the end of a run – and followed his crusty old mate down the darkness of Old Oak Lane to a lodge the old boy said he knew.

At 3 a.m. he was fumbling for the back-door key of a darkened lodging-house, swore, found it and let himself and Ben into a tiny kitchen. Knowing the ropes, the old man stepped over men's traps (bags) but Ben the novice tripped over them and went crashing down bringing saucepans with him as he grabbed for a support. There was no hot water in which to wash himself after shovelling 3 tons of coal into the furnace; he tried to wash in cold, dried himself on a filthy towel, turned down the gas and went upstairs. Heavy snoring came from all rooms but the room where they were to sleep was open and his mate was already down to his long-johns, standing by a single bed squeezed into the remaining space beyond a big double bed where two sooty enginemen were fast asleep. Under the gaslight they looked ghastly and Ben stood in the doorway, mouth open in disbelief. 'Come on,' said his mate, 'this'll do us – they're Weymouth men, they pay sixpence extra for the big bed.' Ben took his top clothes off and climbed into the narrow bed beside the old man in his long-johns. How he snored! And how poor, sensitive Ben lay awake, cold and uncomfortable for what seemed hours on the edge of the bed until sleep finally claimed him.

NINE

The Royal Railway

The Great Western fought a long, losing battle against the encroachments of road transport into its passenger and freight business, the effects of which were seen most readily on the small branch lines built into remote areas during the Second Railway Mania of the mid-nineteenth century. The lines became barely profitable yet many shops, farms and small works depended on them; the Great Western Directors felt they had a public duty to perform and bore the loss. It could be argued that the railways of the West were never so public as when they were privately owned by conscientious proprietors, many of whom lived on the little branch lines. In 1926, H.L. Wilkinson, Assistant to the Superintendent of the Line, was asked to make a survey of six minor branch railways and to report on ways of reducing operating costs and even to see if there was a case for taking up the rails and laying a road for the use of the Company's own motor buses. In his report on the 3½-miles-long Faringdon branch he stated, 'Passengers have to change trains which is inconvenient and gives an advantage to road transport. Goods traffic, especially perishables needing a quick transit, stand on sidings waiting a service on the branch or main line and the station is remote from the village, which was not a disadvantage when the line was built but now gives an advantage to the motor bus. Very little can be done but we will keep an eye on the situation.' An eye was kept on declining returns throughout the life of the Great Western without the line being closed.

In 1927 the Great Western Directors seriously attempted to

modernise the railway by installing electric traction with the
overhead catenary. The intention was to start with the
Paddington–Bicester–Birmingham route where the GWR was
in direct competition with the shorter, and potentially faster,
LMS route from Euston via Bletchley. The scheme did not go
to the drawing-boards because the southern end of the GWR
route was shared by engines from the LNER and Metropolitan.
There were fears for the safety of the line under steam and
electric haulage so attention was turned to the Great Western
route with the highest consumption of coal and the worst
gradients – the Taunton–Penzance line. Not only was the main
trunk to be electrified but every branch line, right down to the
little Hemyock and the Cornish china-clay lines; battery
locomotives would have worked on the docks; and apart from
the curious exception of the 'Cornish Riviera' and the 'Torbay
Express' all trains would have stopped at Taunton to change
engines. Dock engines apart, there were to have been two kinds
of electric locomotive: a general-purpose, 1300-hp machine
running on four axles in a rigid frame or on two four-wheel
bogies; and an express type with a 2–6–2 or 4–6–2 wheel
arrangement producing 2400 hp to drive the wheels through
gearing after the Continental and American models. The GWR
calculated that a 2400-hp machine could haul 514 tons non-
stop from Taunton to Penzance at an average of 57 mph while a
'Castle' could be expected to average 47 mph with 257 tons.
There would have been a combined steam and electric locomotive depot on the downside just west of Taunton station with a
subway from it to the upside, eastern end of the station so that
engine-changing movements would not interfere with traffic.
The plans, sketches and estimates I have seen at Paddington
make no reference to modernising the signalling but as the
Great Western was in the process of planning power signalling
at Paddington, and other schemes following at Bristol, Newport and Cardiff, it seems likely that colour-light signalling
would have followed the catenary westwards from Taunton.
The scheme was abandoned owing to the worsening economic

situation which reached its nadir in the Great Depression of 1929–32. It was revived in 1938 as a simple electrification of the main trunk line west of Taunton but was again abandoned because of the outbreak of war so that the 'Kings' survived to haul me when I was a youngster regularly from Reading to Plymouth in the 1950s.

In 1929 Great Western express trains ran fairly well – often 80 per cent of them arrived at their destination within five minutes of 'time' – but schedules were, with the exception of a few 'hard-hitting' expresses on the Birmingham and west of England lines, easy with plenty of 'recovery time' against the day of poor steaming, overloading or out-of-course delay. The 9.55 a.m. Ilfracombe to Paddington was an example of a good-quality 'A' headcode train – for not all express trains were equal – moderately fast without the flair of the 'Cornish Riviera'. The Ilfracombe was formed with nine coaches from Taunton: five from Ilfracombe, three from Minehead, including a slip coach, and a dining car from the sidings at Taunton. The 'diner' had been on the 7.15 a.m. Paddington to Bristol of the previous day and had been worked down to Taunton from Bristol on the 10.5 a.m. Bath to Taunton stopping train. The slip coach, which was to be dropped off at Reading, had come down the previous day on the back of the 3.30 p.m. Paddington, slipped at Taunton and then worked down to Minehead on the branch train. These 'portions' were amalgamated at Taunton in ten minutes and ran non-stop to Bristol at an average speed of 47 mph over the intervening 44¾ miles. For no discernible reason the train stood in Temple Meads station for fifteen minutes and then set out for Bath, covering the 11½ miles at an average of 43 mph, start to stop – a much harder timing than previously. It then spent nine minutes standing while the train engine went off to fetch a slip coach and a composite class coach off the middle siding, came back and buffered them to the front of the train. This was the slip portion for Bath off the 11.15 a.m. Paddington. Thereafter the train was booked non-stop to Paddington at an average of 56 mph including the 20 mph slowing whilst diverting to the platform loop at Reading where the slip coach was dropped. By 1936 the train was booked to average 51½ mph between Taunton and Bristol including a three-minute call at Highbridge. Average speeds were higher throughout but the slip coach service for Reading was abandoned for a normal call so the train arrived no earlier at Paddington.

While the splendid 'Castle' class engine was sprinting across the Athelney marshes or hammering hard against the collar through Box, the passengers were leaning back luxuriously on Swindon's floral, blue and gold moquette in their snug, solid-looking compartments, perhaps enjoying a three-course meal served on a table there or in the dining car. For 3 shillings they got turbot – if it was Friday – or else roast beef and horse radish sauce, potatoes and cauliflower, fruit and custard, biscuits and cheese with coffee and sweet biscuits to follow. The sweet biscuits were Huntley & Palmer's 'Great Western Selection' from an appropriately lettered tin. Passengers were waited on by waiters in smart livery; they ate off porcelain with silver-plated cutlery; there were silver-plated jugs and cruets, all with the GWR crest. With their meal they could drink GWR wine specially bottled and labelled by the Company or enjoy the 'GWR Special Whisky' which was sold at a shilling for a 'double'. The whisky was blended by the fine firm of Macdonald Greenlees and was so special that a grateful public put away 1000 gallons a year – twenty hogsheads were delivered annually to Paddington where it was bottled and labelled by the Company's Catering Department. Today, the nearest one could get to the quality of the GWR's favourite tipple would be Macdonald Greenlees export whisky 'Old Parr'.

The Great Western was a very *stylish* railway – at its best – rather than a very fast or very modern one. Its trains were tolerably fast, they looked grand and they suited perfectly the countryside through which they ran. Their public was, by 1930, intensely proud of the aristocratic, green and gold, cream and brown expresses; they applauded the daily feats of the

London to Birmingham two-hour trains and the 'Cornish Riviera' and accepted as the natural order of things that there were no express trains between Cheddar and Frome, Minehead and Taunton; these were *branch lines* after all.

In 1929 the Great Western cut the schedule of the 3.45 Swindon to Paddington to seventy minutes and the 'Cheltenham Flyer' was born. Such a deliberate attempt at sustained high speed had not been attempted before in Britain and the public loved it. In the depths of the Great Depression on 14 September 1931 the time was cut to sixty-seven minutes and the inaugural run was in the hands of Jim Street with Fireman Sherer, Jim's regular mate, with 5000 *Launceston Castle*. The train was packed with excited enthusiasts, jumping up and down in the corridors and slapping each other on the backs as each succeeding station was passed at unprecedented speed. The route was lined with cheering spectators. Jim Street and Frank Sherer arrived at Paddington in 59½ minutes and were mobbed by a tumultuous crowd who struggled to shake hands with them, patted the engine as if it were a racehorse and shoved bunches of flowers into the enginemen's grimy hands. The LNER accelerated one of their Grantham–King's Cross trains to beat the 'Flyer's' scheduled, start-to-stop average of 69 mph, whereupon the Great Western, not to be outdone, cut the 'Flyer's' time to sixty-five minutes for the 77¼ miles. The newspapers were full of the 'race'. Stations along the route were daily thronged with boys and girls of all ages eagerly awaiting the thrilling thunder of a 'Castle' notched-up and running fast and the Great Western's publicity department had a field-day. The 2.40 p.m. Cheltenham – or 3.45 p.m. Swindon – was 'The World's Fastest Train' and carried a headboard to say so. The Old Oak men who took the job from those at Swindon, proved it, vied with each other to produce the fastest time up to Town and in *Punch* Bateman drew his famous cartoon of 'The Man Who Pulled the Communication Cord on the "Cheltenham Flyer" '. In one picture the miserable wretch is seen cowering in one corner of his compartment as a huge, red faced, fire-breathing guard prepares to lift him out and in the next the poor devil is seen hanging by the neck from a signal bracket while the other passengers shake their fists at him and even the engine seems to be in a seething fury. The Great Western made good publicity with the 'Flyer' by selling 5-shilling excursion tickets from Paddington so that enthusiasts could ride back on their show train and the drivers and their firemen without fail did their damnedest to give them a treat when speeds of 90–95 mph were maintained for miles.

But any engineman worth his salt would be willing to 'have a go'. On 16 March 1931 British Movietone News made a film of the Great Western's Automatic Train Control equipment in action. A microphone was installed in the cab; the film camera-man squatted behind his camera on its heavy tripod at the back of the tender where a metal floor surrounds the filling hole and kept his head low – there were four inches between the film cans and the underside of bridges. A cable took sound back to a gramophone disc-cutting machine set up in a limousine which was roped to a carriage truck and behind this was a saloon coach for officials. Hauling this distinctive equippage was one of the most famous of Great Western engines, 4073 *Caerphilly Castle*, known to me and to thousands of small boys, affection-ately, as 'Carefully Castle'. The train left Paddington at 9.42 a.m. in bright spring sunshine with a sharp wind blowing – ideal weather for photography but not so good for the camera-man riding on the tender like the travelling porter of old. Distant signals were held at 'Caution' here and there and a good record of the bell, siren and footplate work was made. At Slough the train was stabled to await the 8.34 a.m. express from Plymouth, due at 12.55, for the bright idea had been conceived that an exciting climax to the film could be achieved if the express were filmed thundering up to and overtaking the special.

At 12.50, 4073 was let out onto the up relief line and went on her way at 25 mph with the film camera trained expectantly westwards. Up came the Plymouth, going well, too well. It was overtaking too quickly so a phone call was made to the driver of 4073: 'A bit faster, please.' The request was answered enthusiastically and – uncarefully – *Caerphilly Castle* was unleashed. The cameraman, busy filming, was taken by surprise as his precarious perch surged forward but he maintained his equilibrium professionally and continued to film the race as 4073 set off in hot pursuit of the Plymouth. Bridges began to flick past his left ear, 60 mph in half a mile, 70, 80, catching up, still filming, 81, 82, overtaking and then easing to pace the 'fast', filming the delighted waves of the passengers and the studied indifference of the men on the 'King' as both trains ran neck and neck through the ever more complicated track-work towards Paddington.

The 'dear old Gee-Dub', to use my uncle's affectionate 1930s phrase, was made superbly well, made the best of its essentially pre-war equipment and, through excellent public relations work, made sure the public knew. The times were not easy ones for industry. The Company seemed loth to spend money on new equipment but, hoping for an improvement in national trade, rested on its glossy laurels. There were, however, in the 1930s two great innovations which were stylish, popular and years ahead of their time. On 12 April 1933 the Great Western inaugurated the first internal air service in Britain, carrying passengers and mail to and from Cardiff, Torquay and Plymouth and in 1934 introduced the first diesel rail-cars to run on British tracks. The aeroplanes were three-engined Westland Wessex, owned and flown by Imperial Airways, but painted chocolate and cream, the registration G–A–A–GW on the fuselage and the Great Western coat of arms on the tailplane. The first rail-cars were in sleek imitation of the high-speed diesel train in Germany – the 'Flying Hamburger' (Hamburger having connotations only with that city in those days) – and ran at 75 mph. Later models hauled buffet cars between Birmingham and Cardiff and drummed up so much traffic that the GWR took the somewhat illogical step of replacing them with a steam engine and coaches.

To celebrate the centenary of the Great Western in 1935, a 'Flyer' was put on to run between Paddington and Bristol, 118 miles in 105 minutes. This was the 'Bristolian' which topped 100 mph occasionally, the acme of Great Western perfection with a gleaming 'Castle' and a rake of seven or eight brand-new, cream-and-brown coaches. This spectacular work, as well as the Birmingham 'two-hour' trains and the 'Cornish Riviera', was the up-market end of the Great Western's business, glittering with the old, Imperial grandeur when the country was down in the dumps dazzling all and sundry to the fact that the GWR was really 'marking time'.

In his speech at the Centenary Dinner at Grosvenor House for the Great Western, Edward, Prince of Wales, said, 'I have a personal association with the Great Western Railway because it serves the Duchy of Cornwall where, as Duke of Cornwall, I have many tenants who are dependent on your services. You carry their produce and bring them holiday-makers to some of the most beautiful parts of the British Isles. It is, therefore, not only as a traveller but as a landowner and indeed a customer that I have accepted your hospitable invitation tonight. I wish to pay tribute to all that the Great Western has done for the West Country. Safety, comfort, convenience, punctuality and flexibility have been the keynotes of your administration. You have discharged your honour to the public with loyalty and integrity. You are a venerable and honoured institution in our native land and you well deserve the name, "The Royal Road".'

A fast, frequent train service requires good signalling and though by 1935 the GWR had installed power-operated colour-light systems at Paddington, Bristol and Cardiff, these were not as modern as they seemed. They were, in fact, the old 'block telegraph' system converted to power operations which reduced the number of signal boxes required and made life easier for drivers during fog and took the physical effort out of the signalman's work. They were an improvement but were only a 'half-way house' to truly modern signalling. The rest of the railway was signalled in the traditional way, largely with Victorian equipment which depended for its safe working on hundreds of fine signalmen maintaining the highest standards of personal behaviour when dealing with it.

There were thousands of odd little incidents which affected semaphore signalling safety. A signalman would 'switch out' his signal box – pull the running line signal levers over to lower the semaphores – and then turn the switch so that the boxes on each side with which he normally worked would be in direct contact with each other. He could then go home. The day wore on, the sun got warmer and signal wires expanded. If a wire was only just taut enough to lower the arm when it expanded it would allow the arm to return by that amount towards the horizontal 'Danger' position. Occasionally a signalman would forget to wind his wires up tight after he had pulled the levers over and then the stop signals might slacken off and return to 'Danger' while the 'Distant' signal wire, nice and tight, kept that arm showing 'All Right'. It was known to happen and it gave drivers a nasty shock when it did.

One day in November 1936 Driver Oliver was coming up Dainton bank with the 12.15 a.m. Plymouth mail and passenger train. Dainton's up distant signal was 'off' and so was the 'home' but as he entered the tunnel he saw the red light of the starting signal showing beyond the far end of the hole. He braked hard and stopped a train's length beyond the signal. He sent his fireman back through the tunnel to the signal box to see what was the matter. 'There's nothing the matter,' said the signalman, 'look, the lever is over in the frame and the signal repeater is showing that the arm is "off".'

'Well, I can tell you the arm is on,' replied the fireman emphatically. 'Come and look for yourself.' The signalman did so and was duly amazed to see the red light. Back in the box with the fireman, he tapped the repeater's case. The indication swung over to 'Signal On'. The lever was still pulled over in the frame. 'Try tightening your wire up,' suggested the fireman. That did the trick. What had happened was that the wire was tight enough to lower the arm and to therefore work the repeater in the box when the lever was first pulled but was not taut enough to hold the arm lowered. The indicator in the repeater stuck at 'Signal Off' inside the box while beyond the tunnel the signal arm fell back to 'Danger'.

In September 1936 Driver Pope was running bunker first along the goods loop from Park Junction to Gaer Junction. Halfway along the loop he saw the loop exit signal 'off' so he gently applied steam to pick his train up. A minute later he saw that the catch-point at the end of the loop was open – protecting the main line by facing towards the 'throw-off' position. He quickly brought the train under control and crept right onto the catch, putting one wheel into the open blade so that the signalman could not reverse the points. Then he went into the box to beard the man. The signalman was quite unaware of the situation so Driver Pope phoned Control to report that the signal was 'off' to leave the loop, while the catch points were open to throw the train on the 'Land of My Fathers'. What had happened was that when the signalman replaced the lever working that signal the arm's pivot spindle, bone-dry from lack of oil, remained 'stuck off', though the lever had been replaced back in the frame which released the interlocking to allow the catch point lever to be moved. The signalman got a rocket for not taking proper notice of what he was doing and Driver Pope got 10s 6d for preventing a derailment.

If a semaphore signalman becomes neglectful anything can happen. It was extremely rare for a man to fail but one of those rare occasions took place on 15 January 1936 at Shrivenham about six miles east of Swindon. It was the first serious accident on the Great Western since the Reading job in 1914 and was infinitely more tragic since at Shrivenham there was no confusion just plain neglect of a basic, a sacred, duty of all signalmen: *never* send 'Train out of Section' until one has seen the tail-lamp of the train concerned. The tracks westwards to Marston Crossing box 2½ miles away were double, eastwards to Ashbury Crossing 1122 yds away they were quadruple and from

Ashbury to Knighton they were double but with an up goods loop access to which was controlled either from Shrivenham or Ashbury boxes. Shrivenham's up home signal stood 345 yds west of the box and leading up to it was a 'track circuit' 846 yds long. This electrical device used the rails as conductors for a current which provided an indication in Shrivenham box if a vehicle stood anywhere along its length and, if the 'track' was occupied, the device prevented the Shrivenham signalman from giving a 'Line Clear' indication to Marston Crossing. Without this indication the Marston signalman could not pull the lever controlling the signal which gave access to Shrivenham's section.

The signalman at Shrivenham was fifty-two-years-old Bill Head with thirty-four years' service as a signalman and at Ashbury was Signalman Jefferies, thirty-six years old with nineteen years' service. At 5 a.m. in pitch darkness, patchy fog and a temperature 15°F below freezing, a coal train from Aberdare to Old Oak Common, hauled by 2802, moved gently out of Swindon yard 2½ hours late. It was just the kind of train the Great Western was trying to get rid of. Fifty-three wooden-bodied coal tubs each running on two grease-lubricated axles, carrying 10 tons of coal and coupled with long three-link chains. With the couplings taut the train was 400 yds long, its 1200 tons braked only by the guard's hand-brake and the hand and vacuum brakes on the engine. The power brake was not normally used with such a load, it braked the engine too rapidly and allowed the lumbering, unbraked wagons to run up hard against the tender which could lead to damage and derailment. Driver Davis and Fireman Jenkins were on 2802 which took up the slack couplings so gently that Guard Chapman felt only a slight tug as his van was finally picked up by the engine. Care was essential in starting and running a loose-coupled train to avoid 'snatch' which could break a heavy coupling like cotton thread. (In 1935 1000 couplings and 2700 draw-bars or hooks broke on freight trains throughout Britain.)

At 5.4 a.m., the 9 p.m. Penzance to Paddington – the 'Up

Waker' – consisting of nine of the Great Western's best carriages and sleeping cars, stopped at Swindon dead on time. It
was hauled by 6007 *King William III* with Driver Starr and
Fireman Cozens, both top-link Newton Abbot men working
through to Paddington. All was in order except that the coach
attached at Newton off the Kingswear line had been incorrectly
marshalled next to the tender, the most dangerous place in the
train in the event of an accident while the brake-van, which
ought to have occupied that position, was behind the coach.
Into the leading coach got six passengers, all compartments
were occupied, the leading three or four had not been locked to
leave an empty space between the tender and the passengers.

Number 2802 trudged eastwards at 25 mph, the safe speed
for a 3–4–1 bell code 'H' headcode train. It passed Marston
Crossing box at 5.8. One and a half minutes later, silently and
without any snatch but due entirely to the intense cold acting
on internally flawed metal, the rear drawhook of the forty-
eighth wagon fell apart; the heavy lump of iron dropped onto
the sleepers, five wagons of coal and the guard's van passed over
and left it lying, gathering frost in the dark. On the engine
Davis and Jenkins were anxious about the thick, patchy fog and
kept a sharp look-out forward; in the van Guard Chandler was
anxious not to freeze to death and sat close to his stove. The
track was straight, falling very slightly downhill, the rear six
wagons trundling along, decelerating slowly, the gap between
them and the main train gradually widening until the rear part
came to a stand, without a sound of clashing, closing-up buffers
just 131 yds short of the security of Shrivenham's 'approach
track circuit'.

Ashbury Crossing's distant signal was at 'Caution' below
Shrivenham's home signal. Jenkins knew they were for the loop
and screwed on the engine's hand-brake. The train rolled past
Shrivenham box, wagon buffers ringing as they closed up
against the engine, just as the 1.50 a.m. Kensington to Chippenham milk train went by on the down road, one hour late,
laying a smokescreen for a few seconds between the Aberdare

and Signalman Head. When Head did not see the coal train's triple red tail signal he convinced himself that it was present but obscured by smoke and, instead of doing the usual thing which was to tell his mate at Ashbury what had happened and then wait for the 'Train out of Section' from him, he went against every instinct gained in thirty-four years' service – not to mention the rule-book – and sent the 2 pause 1 bell code 'Train out of Section' to Marston Crossing. He did the same on the down line for the milk empties, having seen its tail lamp and gave 'Line Clear' to Jefferies for a train of empty coaches.

It was 5.15 a.m. The Penzance pulled out of Swindon dead on time. Marston shortly asked the road – 4 beats on the bell – and Bill Head pegged his instrument to 'Line Clear'. All was not lost. The Aberdare was passing Ashbury Crossing box under the watchful gaze of Signalman Jefferies. But Jefferies was not watching, he had his back to the train, having a telephone conversation, the words of which he could not recall later nor the person to whom they were addressed. After the train had passed he looked out, 'thought' he saw a *white* light and on the strength of that sent the fatal 2–1 back to Bill Head whose anxiety promptly vanished. About 960 yds away to the west the missing, triple red tail-lamps burned brightly within a patch of freezing fog while all around was frostily clear. The only man who could then have saved the situation – Guard Chandler – may have been asleep inside his van. At any rate, he sat doing nothing, believing, he said, that the train was at a stand at Shrivenham's up home signal though he had heard none of the prolonged clatter of buffers which ought to have preceded such a stop.

To the rear of the errant brake van, Shrivenham's distant signal was at 'All Right' and the 'King's' ATC bell rang out loud and clear as the engine passed over the ramp at 55 mph. Fireman Cozens stopped firing to 'spot' the home signal which was on his side of the line and saw, mistily through the patch of fog, the terrible red triangle of lights. '*Whoa!*' he yelled just as Driver Starr threw the brake-handle over. Chandler was fated to be a survivor. He had been gassed at Ypres in 1917 and wounded and taken prisoner in March 1918. Now the sound of the express bearing down on him broke through his reveries just in time for him to dive, like a swimmer, head first down the bank as 610 tons travelling at 45 mph collided with 122 tons stationary. The brake-van and nearest three trucks simply disintegrated into a heap of coal and firewood, the furthest two cannoned away up the line. 6007 rode up onto the pile, fell on its right side, Driver Starr's side, and, with him impaled on the handles of the reversing screw, screeched along the rails of the down line for 87 yds. The shock of the blow crushed the leading coach, killing one and injuring ten and even in the rearmost carriage the guard, sitting, sorting letters, was thrown off his seat.

Bill Head saw and heard his up distant signal lever shake and rattle followed by a noise like distant thunder. Knowing that he had not seen the Aberdare's tail-lamp and having gone against all his better judgement in sending that 2–1 to Marston, the sudden, sharp noise from that lever filled him with a sudden, fearful, stomach-churning dread – and now there was the empty coaching stock train on the down line. He was in an agony of shock and indecision. If that noise meant what he knew it must mean he ought to throw his down line signal levers to 'Danger' at once, but then, if he was mistaken, if there was nothing wrong, how would he explain stopping the down train? He stood for a full ninety seconds wondering whether to admit to himself that he had caused a train smash. Jefferies had sent the down train 'on line'; it had already passed Head's distant signal. Head threw the signals to 'Danger' in front of it and as he did so two coal tubs rolled steadily past on the up line, silent and accusing. For Bill Head they may as well have been bats out of hell. He fell into his chair and it was eleven minutes before he had recovered sufficiently to stand and send the 'Obstruction Danger' signal – six beats on the bell – to Ashbury and Marston.

The crash occurred at a very awkward spot on a bank remote

from roads and the under-developed rescue services of the time had a very hard task getting people out of the wreck and away to hospital. Driver Starr 'suffered in the bitter cold with great fortitude' for two hours before they could get him off the handles of the reversing screw and he died there, on the trackside, at fifty-two years of age after thirty-eight years on the Great Western. The uninjured passengers were taken back to Swindon where they had to buy their reviving tots of brandy in the station refreshment room. Some of them wrote to complain about this deplorable lapse in Great Western good manners and as a result Sir James Milne, the General Manager, issued formal instructions that, in any future, similar, situation, brandy was to be given free of charge to shocked survivors. I do not know what became of Bill Head or whether Fireman Cozens continued on the footplate but Jefferies was posted to Radstock, presumably as a punishment, where he spent the last twenty-five years of his railway service as a signalman – and on a single track at that.

TEN

The Great Western at Dunkirk

Signalmen had no formal training for their highly responsible work but cleaners and young firemen could learn their art through the work of volunteers running each engine shed's Mutual Improvement Class (MIC). At Oxford shed the classroom was a grounded coach body and throughout the 1930s and 1940s, if not earlier, the principal instructor (though he would have denied it) was Albert King. He was a born teacher from a totally pastoral background; his paternal grandfather was the miller of Arncott near Bicester and his maternal grandfather was a shepherd on the Quantock Hills. His parents were both 'soldiers' in the Salvation Army so he was a good musician and with this talent, keen intelligence and varied antecedents he became an engine cleaner on Oxford shed in June 1915 aged fifteen. He worked a 72-hour week for a shilling a day until October 1916 when, tired of the long hours and drudgery of the shed, he decided to escape to the army. This was probably the only really thoughtless thing he did in his life but he survived eighteen months of extremely long and uncomfortable hours, not to mention the very large risk of a sudden and violent death and returned to Oxford shed where he shortly became a fireman.

He was a slim, studious and quite monastically shy person, a 'scholar' rather than a fireman, though he was very good at his job because he took such an interest in its skills and complications. His academic character found outlet in becoming a lecturer for the shed MIC and even old-hand drivers would come into class when it was Albert's evening to give a talk. His shyness was well known. One day when he was off duty, his driver took Len Wheeler for fireman to Paddington. Waiting there for the return trip the driver got down to the track for a final look-round the engine and when he got back onto the footplate all he could see of Len was the seat of his overalls as he leaned enthusiastically out over the cabside, talking to a couple of pretty girls. The girls left to board the train and Len turned into the cab. 'Ha!' exclaimed his mate. 'Easy to see Albert's not here. If them two had turned up with him on the engine he'd have been down on the track with me in a flash.'

Albert worked like a missionary for the ideal of Mutual Improvement and travelled round to small depots such as Fairford or Honeybourne to give talks illustrated with lantern slides supplied by Swindon factory, with models of valve gears or injectors, sectioned to show their operation. The models were made by Driver 'Doc' Wall of Oxford and Horace Tolley, a non-railwayman who lived near Albert in Botley Road. Other enthusiasts wrote MIC textbooks. Ernie Nutty of Swindon works' drawing office wrote a classic of clarity, *GWR Two-Cylinder Locomotives*; C.H. Mather of Port Talbot produced an excellent book on the GWR vacuum-brake and A.E. (Algy) Hunt did a rather scruffy book, *The Locomotive*, which nevertheless sold over 13,000 copies. Railwaymen were keen to learn about their work, signalmen and clerks bought textbooks written by Inspectors on signalling rules, and most Great Western men felt a strong commitment to and interest in 'The Job'. This state of mind, which I have personally experienced, has been acknowledged to me, quite unprompted, in correspondence with old-hand signalmen, drivers and a retired Locomotive Superintendent of the Great Western – and its existence was universally acknowledged to stem from the presence at the heart and core of the railway of the magnificent, dirty and much-respected steam engines.

Algy Hunt became an engine cleaner on Oxford shed in 1911, went to Oswestry for his first firing job in 1925 and there became a leading figure in the local MIC movement. By 1935 he and Albert King were travelling around Great Western territory and beyond in Algy's Austin 7 car, using their own time and money to give lectures at small sheds and to build the Mutual Improvement movement on the Great Western and other railways in conjunction with those local stalwarts throughout the country. In 1937 they were able to hold the first, national Conference of the Federation of Mutual Improvement Classes for the purpose of 'improving the technical training of enginemen and perfecting the means by which this may be done'.

About 1940, Algy seriously injured his leg and was sent from Oswestry to the Radcliffe Infirmary, Oxford, for treatment after which he was posted to Oxford shed as a driver. He and Albert, who was then on permanent early turn on the shed because he was in charge of the railway Home Guard, worked hard at the MIC together. They made an odd pair in harness: Algy, a big man, already inclined to be stout, cheerful if somewhat self-important, married, good with machinery; Albert, ascetic-looking, artistic and considered somewhat eccentric – though this was only the result of an inquiring mind, such as the period when he attached a device to his leg, a home-made pedometer, so that he could measure the miles he walked around the shed. He was a confirmed bachelor, wedded to the job, his voluntary organisations and to evenings spent making and firing high-quality pottery. About 1942 Algy decided it was time to jolly him along so he invited a nurse he had got to know from his long stay in the Radcliffe to join Albert, Mrs Hunt and himself in a river cruise in his motor-boat *Lavengro*. A picnic was prepared and the party set off up-stream, through the wide, sunny expanse of Port Meadow – with Albert sitting unhappily in the pointed end looking like a stranded fish. He had taken fright when he saw there was an unattached female in the party and the man, who could draw a crowd to listen to his erudite lectures on such delightful subjects as superheaters, remained in the sharp end of the boat and uttered barely a word throughout the trip.

One of Albert's most attentive pupils was a cleaner of engines, Charlie Turner. They were both enthusiasts for 'The Job' and indeed it seemed highly appropriate that the University town's engine shed should have had such dedicated teachers and devoted students. Charlie genuinely liked steam engines, dirt and all. He was fifteen in 1931, too young to enter the engine shed, so he took a 'grease-monkey's' job with the promise of a transfer to the shed on his sixteenth birthday. He worked with the Carriage & Wagon Examiner from his lair by the old North box, opposite the shed yard, close enough to keep his enthusiasm alight while he was stuffing axle-boxes with yellow fat. The majority of wagons then, particularly 'private owner' wagons ran on primitive 'grease-boxes' which had to be examined for overheating and given fresh lubricant every 60 miles during their slow perambulations of the countryside.

The 'star turn' of Charlie's day was the 11.30 a.m. Bordsley–Southall 'Long Tom': one hundred loaded, wooden coal tubs running on 400 grease-lubricated bearings behind an 'Aberdare' 2–6–0 or '28' class 2–8–0 engine. The train left the loop at Astrop, Banbury, at 3.42 p.m. behind a Birmingham–Oxford stopping passenger train and ran into the loop at Wolvercote Junction, Oxford, at 4.20, 17½ miles further on. The lumbering train kept good time because it had to, there were no intermediate refuges long enough to accommodate it should it run late and a following train wish to pass. It arrived at the Oxford North box end of the loop at 4.40, the tail stretching back to the Hayfield Road bridge. In warm weather all the boxes were dripping grease and most needed refilling so the half-hour allowed for examination was none too long and there would be a rush to finish for it was most important that the train kept to its booked path. The 'Salop parcels' left Oxford twenty minutes behind it and the 3.40 Malvern–Paddington was behind that over the refuge-less 11 miles to Didcot. The Malvern was 'non-stop London in the hour', one of the fastest trains on the GWR.

Charlie moved to the engine shed in 1932 and did his share of labouring jobs besides cleaning engines, the latter having become, by then, what the old hands called a 'wipe it over' job. He did his first turn of real firing while still a cleaner with Driver Fred Richards. The train was the 3.42 'all stations' to Worcester, 5063 *Earl Baldwin* was the appropriately named engine and the coal was 'nutty slack'. Luckily Fred was an intelligent driver, the engine steamed freely, Charlie was strong and willing so that the passengers got to their destinations on time and Charlie got to Worcester somewhat fagged but feeling so pleased with himself that he hardly noticed.

The outcome would have been much different if the dreaded Ern Gable had been driving. Ern was a 'thrasher' of engines, an un-subtle man. When war was declared on 3 September 1939 very heavy traffic promptly appeared on the railways. On the 4th the Great Western ran 320 troop trains, 350 stores and ammunition trains and several carrying meat and butter from the London docks for dispersal in cold stores around the country. Shortly after this 330 specials took thousands of children from major cities to country areas to escape the bombing and gas attacks that were daily expected. Charlie and Ern Gable had to work a '63' class engine with an eight-coach special for Reading and London only as part of this vast, logistical miracle. While they were standing at the up platform at Oxford, Ern was grumbling about 'young-hand firemen' – meaning Charlie – and finally went across to the Goods Shed box (later Oxford Station South) to phone the shed and complain. The signals were 'off' for the train to leave but that did not worry Gable. The engine was roaring away at the safety-valves because Charlie had prepared his fire for a punctual departure – no matter. Finally Ern arrived back on the engine and without a word flung up the regulator and off they went. Thrash, thrash, thrash. No thought of pulling up the reversing lever as he rummaged about in the tool box looking for his pipe and tobacco. When the pipe was lit the engine was adjusted. All the way to London that was how it was, fire dancing on the bare firebars, Charlie sweating away trying to

throw coal in fast enough to keep up and all totally unnecessary.

They came back 'on the cushions' and Gable chose a compartment already occupied by two soldiers. There being a war
on soldiers were popular and Charlie could see that Ern was
dying to talk to them. At last he blurted out 'I'm Ern Gable –
my boy's in the army – do you know him?' The soldiers had to
admit they did not and as the incredulous Gable quizzed them,
Charlie squirmed with embarrassment for his mate's ignor-
ance. Just as it was unthinkable that Charlie should have
interfered with the running of the engine, no matter how badly
Ern was driving, so it was unthinkable that Charlie should have
got up and left his mate in the compartment. At last they
reached Oxford, they could book off and Charlie could escape.
As they walked along the platform towards the shed, Ern Gable
put his arm round Turner's shoulder, gave him a squeeze and
said, 'There – no one can say now that Ern Gable's scared of
taking a young-hand with him.'

Railway work was again a business of very long hours as it
had been in 1914, though in 1940 ambulance trains gave three
days' rather than three hours' notice of their arrival and when
Charlie was called-up into the Railway Operating Division of
the Royal Engineers he, like Albert King before, felt glad of the
chance to escape into a better ordered world. The last trip he
did before reporting for duty at Longmoor was with Driver
'Gentleman' Jim Honey and as they booked off together, the
ROD veteran shook hands warmly with his young fireman and
wished him well. The Royal Engineers had gained another,
highly competent, Great Western Railway engineman.

He was called-up on 15 February 1940, did basic weapon-
training and technical training on the Westinghouse brake and
other companies' locomotives and on 10 May he was given a
week's leave prior to going with his Company, 191 ROD, to join
the fray in France. The speed of the German army's advance,
assisted largely by German dive-bombers, took everyone by
surprise, including, obviously, the department of the War

Office responsible for postings. France had all but been overrun by the time Charlie came off leave so instead of France he went to Inverness and spent several idyllic months riding about on 'Loch' and 'Ben' class engines, learning the road between Inverness and Thurso.

The Germans had swept aside all opposition and by 23 May 1940 their army was pinning large numbers of Allied soldiers against the sea. Calais and Boulogne fell but at Dunkirk large flooded areas lay across the Germans' path which enabled the British rearguard to form a fiercely held perimeter which was only forced in very slowly while the defenders placed a blind faith in the ability of the Royal Navy to rescue them. The Royal Navy did and to help them in the task of evacuating the men they enlisted the help of – amongst that of many others – the ships and men of the Great Western Railway. The passenger ferries, *St Andrew*, *St Julien* and *St David*, re-painted white with red crosses as hospital ships, had been working across the Channel since the war began so their crews were tired before they started the constant shuttle from Dover to Dunkirk. The Channel Islands freighters, *Roebuck* and *Sambur*, were requisitioned for the evacuation without even 'de-gaussing' so that their crews sailed through waters strewn with magnetic mines in un-demagnetised ships.

The narrow sea was like a traffic jam of ships: lines of Thames pleasure-boats tied together like corks on a string, towed by a larger ship; warships, tugs, private yachts – all plunging along as fast as they could go, nose to tail. The GWR's Channel Islands passenger ferry *St Helier* was crowded so close by a following destroyer as they tore around the buoy to enter the Dunkirk roads that her stern was scraped by the warship's bows. The three GWR ferries used as hospital ships were particularly sought out and attacked by the German planes and land batteries. They carried no medical staff and when they docked in the smoking, blazing town the crew went ashore with stretchers to carry wounded men into the ship under gunfire from nearby buildings. The sleepless strain was enormous . On

29 May Captain Joy of *St David* collapsed on the bridge to be replaced by his 1st Officer, Mr Mendus, and in Dover the same day *St David*'s 2nd Officer was found wandering about the town lost, suffering from amnesia.

As the Dunkirk defensive perimeter contracted the Germans were able to place field-guns near the beaches to harass the ships as they sailed north between sandbanks and the coast, parallel to the beaches. This closed the short (39 sea miles) route from Dover and forced rescuers to take the northerly, 87-mile passage. In the shallow, narrow, sea lanes on the landward side of the sandbanks masking Dunkirk, ships such as *St David* or *St Helier* had little room to zigzag to avoid bombs and in any case, such manoeuvres were dangerous with so many other craft crowding the water. Captain Pitman of *St Helier* survived days of aerial attack by 'steering towards the spot where the last bomb fell' thus, through columns of spray, strained in the hull by huge explosions within 20 ft of her bows, the gallant ship would push her bows into the smoking ruin of Dunkirk harbour to lie alongside the crumbling jetty to embark another 2000 men.

On the evening of 28 May a terrific air raid was in progress as *St Helier* set out full speed for England with 2000 French troops on board. The minesweeper HMS *Sharpshooter*, crossing her path, was struck, the steel bows of the Great Western ship biting deep into the wooden naval vessel. To have backed off would have resulted in the sinking of *Sharpshooter* so *St Helier* ploughed on with the minesweeper stuck onto her bows at right angles. After forty minutes a tug came to the rescue and took *Sharpshooter* in tow; *St Helier* made way again and was promptly run into by an ancient paddle-steamer, *Princess Eleanor*, which never faltered in her furious passage for France but left her starboard paddle-box hanging over the bows of *St Helier*. The 'passengers' and crew saw the lights of Dover coming up, relaxed slightly only to be thrown all over the ship as it lifted out of the water, listed to port and with terrifying grinding noises grated the length of her keel over the wreck. *St*

Helier and her crew worked to the end, the ship down at the bows from a leaking hull, and had the honour to carry the last contingent of men before the Senior Naval Officer signalled 'BEF Evacuated' to the Admiralty. The ship had carried 11,700 people in eight successful trips – many more runs never made a landfall owing to the intense German gunfire. Captain Pitman, his 1st and 2nd Officers were awarded the DSC and the ship's Quartermaster the DCM for their part in an operation which Mr Churchill had hoped would lift 30,000 men but in fact saved 337,000 in what he called 'a miracle of deliverance' when 'only the most reckless, expert, daring of men willing and able to give whatever the moment might call for was able to wring success from a situation which embodied every element of disaster'.

After Dunkirk the fear of invasion was everywhere – well, almost. On Oxford shed, where the men were bound by a communal self-discipline and camaraderie which perhaps did not bear on 'the man in the street', life went on with cheerful perseverance. Albert King had undertaken the formation of a Home Guard unit and fire-watching patrol and was on permanent early turn in the shed to be able to administer it. His command consisted of 130 volunteers, one Lee-Enfield rifle and four 20-mm anti-aircraft cannon. No one recalls firing them but there were some wonderful trips down to Poole harbour to practise firing similar guns – and a glorious booze-up afterwards, before setting out for home. The armoury of small arms was doubled by the acquisition of one Canadian Lee-Enfield. Signalmen between Banbury and Oxford had seen it lying in a truck of rubbish and passed the word on so that Albert was able to retrieve it when the train arrived in the loop at Oxford North. It seemed too good to be true, Albert took out the bolt and looked into the barrel – it was blocked. Canadian Lee-Enfields were .300 and someone had loaded it with British .303 ammunition. There was a bullet jammed up the spout. Not to be disappointed, Albert gave it to Horace Tolley who managed to clear the round and the rifle was later fired successfully on the ranges at Churn, beside the Didcot, Newbury and Southampton line.

The Home Guard 'barracks' was a passenger brake-van stabled in the West Midland sidings and from there each evening, after a day's work, the sentries set out to patrol the station area, alert for fire, German paratroopers, spies and other undesirables. Ern Gable was on sentry-go one night on Walton Well bridge, it was his turn for the rifle and he paced up and down with it on his shoulder – on guard. Out of the darkness emerged a total stranger who asked for a light for his fag. Ern's matches were in his trousers. 'Here, hold this,' he said, handing half his command's weaponry to a stranger, 'I can't get me matches out.' Each morning Albert paraded his men in the van and they unloaded the two rifles. It took eleven pushes and ten pulls of the bolts to empty each magazine before the trigger was clicked to de-cock the bolt and there were a lot of little holes in the floor and roof of that van to testify to the sleepy, early morning arithmetic of the men. Though the 20-mm cannon were never fired, a silver and black Messerschmitt 109, shot down by other guns, crashed under the muzzles of the Great Western cannon at the north end of the engine shed yard. The plane remained for some time and, as Albert said, 'made our guns look quite fierce'. I asked him if it had been a 'hit and run' raider. 'Less of a raider – more of a lost sheep,' chuckled the shepherd's grandson.

With *St Andrew* and *St David* away from Fishguard on war work, the aptly named *St Patrick* – no longer needed for the Channel Islands ferry – was put onto the Irish run, bringing over to Fishguard much urgently needed food and manpower. She was armed but it still required the bravest of men and women to work across the south Irish Sea – to a time-table. Three times the ship was attacked by planes and three times she fought them off with her gun but on 13 June 1941, in sight of Fishguard, she took a bomb amidships, broke up and sank in six minutes with the loss of thirty lives including her Master, Captain J. Faraday, and his son. Mary Owen, a stewardess, was awarded the George Cross and Lloyd's Medal for bravery in assisting passengers off the rapidly sinking ship and the 2nd Engineer, F.J. Purcell, and the wireless operator, N.W. Campbell, won the Lloyd's Medal for gallantry at sea. Between September 1939 and March 1945 the GWR lost eighty vessels to enemy action and suffered 250 crashes of German and Allied planes onto its tracks.

German raids were a daily and nightly occurrence in the West Country during 1940–3. At night a strict black-out was kept but signalmen could not extinguish signal lamps nor could enginemen prevent their locomotive's fire from shining like a searchlight and illuminating the clouds of exhaust to make a fiery trail easy for any pilot to see. On moonlit nights the steel rails shone like direction arrows and lone raiders would prowl low, following the tracks, looking for a suitable target. Signalmen along the line would warn each other as the plane flew onwards – 'Look out, there's one about' and the men would leave their boxes to lie out in the field as the deliberately weird, undulating roar of the 'out of synch' twin-engined Messerschmitt 110 rose to a crescendo till the plane flashed past, silvery above the Somerset fields.

At 9 p.m. on 7 October 1941, the great conurbation of Shepton Mallet was attacked. The Germans decided the town was of strategic importance as the single-track Great Western line from Witham to Yatton passed just south of the town running east/west and the double-track Somerset & Dorset lay to the east, running north/south and beside all this there was a lot of valuable milk in the dairies of the metropolis. They duly dispatched a bomber with a great big landmine which they dropped by parachute onto the unsuspecting town just as the pubs were getting busy. Fortunately the breeze was on our side and took the mine to the Great Western embankment, three-quarters of a mile east of the station. The embankment took the blast and saved the town, though the aptly named 'Bulleymore bridge' was blown away and such a crater was made that it took twelve days to fill.

On 4 May 1942 the sirens sounded in Exeter at 1.40 a.m. howling high and low, a blood-chilling sound, well remembered by all who heard it. Railwaymen at St David's station ran to their shelters. One of these of brick with a concrete roof stood opposite the East signal box, 80 ft away across the tracks. Eight men filed in through the narrow door and the last called up to the signalman, Ralph Hamilton, urging him to come down and shelter with the rest. Ralph called back to say he would be all right in the signal box. The raid began with a blaze of magnesium flares, dropping slowly on parachutes as the droning of the bombers mingled menacingly with the wailing of the warning sirens. Some flares landed in a thick, tall holly hedge in a field across the river from the signal box; the entire line of trees burst into flame and the bomb-aimers, thinking some important target had been struck, let their bombs go in that direction. Among the projectiles was a mine which landed on the roof of the shelter opposite East box. There was a blinding, deafening flash-bang and the shelter with eight men vanished leaving only a huge crater in the soft ground. East signal box remained standing, its windows and instruments shattered by the blast and the steel, sentry-box-like shelter in which Hamilton had taken shelter was crushed sideways. Trapped inside Ralph lay as if in some medieval instrument of torture, unable to sit, stand or lie and listened to the thunderous explosions, the whistle of more bombs for the full eighty minutes of the raid. But when he was released he stepped out – painfully stiff but unharmed.

An extremely vicious attack took place in daylight at Castle Cary on 3 September 1942. At 9.14 a.m., the station staff were cheerfully working on the shunting of their yard, using the Yeovil–Durston 'Fly'. Tank-engine 1729 was standing on the up main line, near the signal box, waiting for orders for the next move, the signalman leant on his levers, all was peace. At 9.15 a.m. four high-explosive bombs from a Junkers 88 came whistling down with pinpoint accuracy. One went through the roof of the signal box, reducing it to a pyramid of rubble, and blasting the goods shed behind away; another chewed up 1729 and the other two demolished the station hotel and other buildings at the east end of the layout. In seconds the rural junction became a shambles of craters, torn-up track and shattered buildings. Six people were killed including the signal-man, Mr Silbey, and Mr Shergold, driver of 1729. Work to clear the line began at once with the assistance of 82 Company, Royal Pioneer Corps, who, with their Commanding Officer at their head, had double-marched from Alford camp, three miles away as soon as they heard the noise of the attack. Rubble was filled into craters, 1729 was craned away, tracks relaid and by 11 p.m. that same day trains were passing towards Weymouth on a single track. A small, wooden signal box was rushed down from Reading signal works and by 11.20 a.m. next day normal working was restored. Six men dead for absolutely nothing at all.

The Germans tried, where possible, to increase the blast of their bombs by dropping them on gas works close to the main target and on 27 July 1942 they came all the way from France to try their luck in a dawn raid on the railway complex at Swindon. They brought some 1000-lb bombs with them and aimed a 'stick' of five at the engine shed with the gas works behind – a wide, long target, just right for a line of bombs – but the aimer must have been cross-eyed because they fell into a narrow strip of open ground between the gas works and No 24 carriage shop, then in use for the manufacture of artillery shells. The ground was yards deep in old clinker from locomotives' fireboxes so that, although the explosions were enormous, they came from well below ground-level and the blast therefore rose upwards rather than extending with great force sideways. This minimised damage, No 24 shop was de-roofed, a gas-oil pipe-line was severed and one gas-holder set on fire though the gasworks continued to operate. Elsewhere the yards were bombed. Soft ground prevented much damage but wagons were thrown through the air – it was a damn nuisance.

At 6.45 a.m. they all flew away and during their unimpeded

flight back to France one pilot with a few rounds left in his guns after machine-gunning the gasworks let fly at the stately 2947 *Madresfield Court* as it ran 'light engine' past Yarnbrook box heading for Westbury. Two holes were torn in the cabside sheets rendering the driver and fireman furious but intact. The driver, a veteran of the First World War swore: 'If we'd had a Lewis gun on the back of the tender, I'd have shot the bastard down!'

ELEVEN

End of an Era

Air raids or the bombed-out state of marshalling yards forced 'Control' to park freight trains nose to tail in goods loops out along the line and it became commonplace for men to sit for eight hours on their engine in a loop, go home for rest and return to the same engine in the same loop. The long loop from Ashbury to Knighton Crossing, miles from the necessities of life, soon became known to the permanent-way men and locomen as 'shit-house creek', for obvious reasons. Jack Ody, an Oxford driver, going north on 14 November 1940, never got beyond Leamington and spent the night in the station there, listening, with his fireman to the dreadful thunder of bombs and gunfire from the north-west and watching in fearful silence the weaving of searchlight beams and the flash of explosions as the orange glow spread ever wider across the sky. 'That must be Coventry,' whispered Jack's mate, awe-struck. Forty-five years later Jack could still recall their chastened feelings from that night.

Harry Keen was a guard at Oxford during the war and recalled to me: 'The closer you got to Birmingham the worse it got. It wasn't so bad in the dark, I didn't mind the bits of shrapnel pinging down on the roof of my van or the sound of planes or the thump of the bombs but what got me was when they dropped those flares – they came down in bunches, far brighter than street lamps and I felt as naked as a robin.' Harry was in the loop between Astrop and Banbury on 3 October 1940 when the Germans attacked – as it appeared to him – the gasworks opposite Banbury South signal box. The unholy racket of exploding bombs and machine-gun fire combined with the roar and snarl of aero engines over the fields bathed in a weird light of flames and flares. Harry took it all in his stride and sat puzzling why they were so keen on the gasworks rather than the strategic junctions north and south of the station, but then he reflected that they were only foreigners after all – and waited patiently for them to go away.

Delays to trains were enormous and the strain on wives as they waited all night for their husbands to come home must be recorded. Bert Bourton, an Oxford driver, said good-bye to his wife Vi on the evening of New Year's Day 1941, cycled down Morrell Avenue, over the peaceful Cherwell at Magdalen bridge and up the stately High to book on at the shed for 8 p.m. He was to relieve a train of tanks (armoured fighting vehicles) which was standing in Port Meadow loop on the LMS line into town. The train was for Pembroke Dock. He, his fireman and Harry Keen were to take it to Cardiff. They set off at 9 p.m. and did not do so badly though air raids were never far away. Bristol and Newport were burning as they passed but they covered the 104 miles to Cardiff in 7½ hours, arriving in the Welsh capital to find the station somewhat cratered and the town in flames. In spite of the night's blitz there was a fresh engine and men to take the train on. Bert took his LMS 2–8–0 on shed and the three Oxford men took the first east-bound train home which turned out to be the 9.30 a.m. bound for Bristol. The City of Merchant Adventurers had had its fair share of the Luftwaffe's attention but the service was maintained somehow and after twenty-four hours away Bert came cycling back along the High, past the Cape of Good Hope pub and into his house in Cross Street where Vi was anxiously waiting for him. He was exhausted and she was ready with her stock restorative – egg, milk and brandy whip – which he sipped in his chair by the fire while she set about cooking a meal – and there was little enough food for that under the rationing system. So it went on, day and night for years, and without several thousand like Vi to look after the enginemen, wash and cook for them, the trains on which the war effort depended would have ground to a halt.

Long hours and lack of food sound like a recipe for disaster but the great majority of railwaymen and women worked with great accuracy and on the Great Western there were very few crashes in spite of the potentially lethal combination of exhausting hours, heavy traffic and black-out conditions at night. On 4 November 1940, Driver Stacey, whose house in Acton had been bombed a few days before, and Fireman Seabridge booked on at Old Oak Common shed to work the 9.50 p.m. Paddington to Penzance as far as Plymouth. Their engine was 6028 *King George VI* and the load was thirteen coaches and 900 passengers, including many naval personnel. Bombing took place while they were in Temple Meads station which may have been particularly disturbing for Stacey; anyhow, the train was delayed and arrived in Taunton, on the down relief line, sixty-eight minutes late at 3.30 a.m.

All signals for main and relief lines westwards were at 'Danger' when Stacey ran in on 6028 because Signalman Wadham in West Station box could see a 'situation' developing. The 9.50 p.m. Paddington was scheduled to go away from relief to main line but the 12.50 a.m. Paddington to Penzance newspaper train, non-stop through Taunton on the down main, had been 'wired' as 'five early Westbury' and was now 'getting handy'. Wadham waited, leaning on his levers, watching the clock, waiting to see if the 9.50 Paddington would finish its station work in time to be allowed out, as booked, main line. At 3.36 a.m. he phoned Athelney box, 8 miles away. 'Got the Papers about, Bob?'

'Be by me in one,' came the surprising reply. 'The 12.50 was still picking up time. 'Let him run', thought Wadham to himself and asked the road for the 9.50 down the relief line. He had just finished pulling the appropriate levers over when the signalman at Taunton East Junction asked the road down the main for the 12.50 Paddington. Wadham had first to get the road from West Junction before he could give the road to East Junction but then, from Cogload Junction 4¾ miles to the east

to Norton Fitzwarren 2 miles to the west, red lights changed to
green and amber distant signal lights below them also went to
green – except that on the relief line at Norton Fitzwarren the
signals remained at 'Danger'.

Stacey got the 'right away' at 3.43. He could not see the
junction signal to his left at the platform end because of the
length of the boiler but he could see the other signals away
down the track, double green lights on main and relief lines,
and because he was scheduled to go out main line into his head
came the fixation that he was signalled out onto the down main
line. He whistled-up on 6028 and set sail along the down relief
line. The 12.50 a.m. Paddington was flying down the main
between Cogload and Creech.

Stacey, inexplicably, was unaware of his situation. The line
ahead was virtually straight and the well-spaced green lights of
the relief and main lines shone brightly in the dark until the
length of the boiler obscured the relief line signal at close range.
Norton Fitzwarren's distant signal was at 'Caution' and gave
him a siren 1677 yds before the throw-off points at the end of the
relief line. He cancelled the siren and continued to accelerate.
Signalman Tucker in Silkmill signal box was treated to the
sight of the 'King'-hauled passenger train thundering down the
slow line and the Papers, also 'King'-hauled with a mere five
vans on, coming up on the 9.50's tail on the main line. It never
occurred to him that the 9.50 was speeding somewhat considering that the end of its track was only 1000 yds away.

Bill Coles at Norton lowered his down relief line home signal
when the 'approach track circuit' indicator swung round to
'Occupied'. To his utter amazement the 9.50 went tearing past
as if it had the road to Plymouth as the 12.50 went by on the
main line. 6028 *King George VI*, weighing 89 tons, jumped a
ditch and fell on the fireman's side in a field beyond the
throw-off points. A rivet-head from its bogie-frame shot, bullet-
like, through the side of the fourth van of the 12.50 and the rear
guard's van drew clear with flying ballast rattling hard against
its walls. The leading coaches of the 9.50 telescoped against the

tender, the others scattered fanwise across the tracks as the 12.50's tail-lamp disappeared around a bend. Guard Baggot on the 12.50 was alarmed by the hammering of the stones against his van and applied the brake but neither he nor Driver Hawkins nor Fireman Lindsey had any idea of their narrow escape until they were told by the signalman at Victory Siding box where they were stopped. Twenty-six people on the 9.50 p.m. Paddington were killed, including Fireman Seabridge on whom the engine fell, and fifty-six more were injured.

Driver Stacey was either dog-tired or dozing or so distracted by his own problems as to amount to the same thing but on 2 July 1941, at Dolphin Junction, Signalman Welch, with fifteen years' experience, was thrown off mental balance by his own sense of responsibility. Dolphin Junction signal box was on the north side of a four-track railway, almost 17½ miles from Paddington. Langley box was 1¼ miles to the east and Slough East box was barely 1 mile to the west. The box controlled a double junction thus:

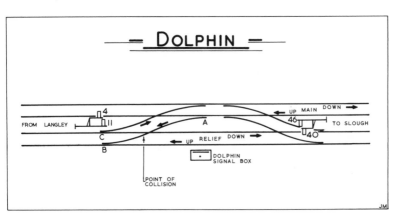

A particular point to remember when operating the box was to be certain to protect crossing movements. For instance, if points A/B were reversed for a train to go from up main or up relief line it was essential that point C was also reversed to divert a train which might run past signals 11/4 at 'Danger'.

The night of 1/2 July 1941 was very hot, the dimly lit interior of Dolphin Junction box was stifling and Welch had opened the windows at each end against the black-out regulations which required all windows to be covered by black cloth or paper with only a small opening at each end to enable the signalman to see trains' tail lamps. It was an impracticable instruction at the best of times and on such a sultry night, with trains running busily, the heat inside the box was more than he could bear. At 2.38 a.m. Signalman Woodhouse in Slough East asked the road up the main line for a train of Government Stores – 4–1 beats on the bell. Welch gave the road, asked on to Adams at Langley and pulled off his signals up the main line.

The Government Stores train passed Slough East at 2.46 p.m. and Woodhouse sent the 'Train entering Section' code to Dolphin. Welch answered this just as Adams at Langley asked the road on the down relief line for the 1.30 a.m. Old Oak Common freight – 3–4–1 beats on the bell. Welch asked the road to Slough East for this train, pulled over his levers and then answered his phone which had been ringing all the while. It was Woodhouse at Slough East who said, 'That 4–1 up the main is terrible, crawling along and the 6.20 Plymouth's getting handy – 2.32 Reading.'

Welch was mortified. He had forgotten the Plymouth – it was thirty minutes late – otherwise he would not have allowed the Government Stores train to run up the main but would have diverted it to the up relief line. The next place able to divert the Government Stores train was West Drayton, 4½ miles, thirteen minutes away for the crawling goods. The Plymouth express would be delayed and he, Welch, would have to answer for it. He was annoyed with himself and an obstinate mood came over him compounded of panic and professional pride. He was not thinking clearly, perhaps because of the oppressive atmosphere inside the dim-lit box in those weary, small hours. He was determined to salvage the situation and wondered if he could cross the Plymouth express to the up relief line – even though such a move was against the rules and common sense in view of the fact that he had given 'Line Clear' for the 3–4–1 to pass on the down relief line.

Instead of instantly replacing the signals to 'Danger' on the down relief line he left them and tried to phone Southall, 8 miles to the east, to make sure the up relief line was clear of freights so that the Plymouth would get a clear run and thus successfully overtake the crawling Government Stores. He waited until 2.49 without getting any answer when the signalling bells called him away from the telephone. Adams at Langley was asking the road down the main for a '5 bells' – a fast goods. Welch gave him the road, sent 'Train entering Section' for the Government Stores lumbering past on the up main and sent 'Train out of Section' for it to Slough East. Woodhouse promptly asked the road for the Plymouth – 4 beats on the bell – and Welch gave the road. He then went back to his pointless research into whether the up relief line was clear when nothing had used that line for over an hour – and still the signals were 'off' on the down relief line.

The Plymouth express, hauled by 4091 *Dudley Castle*, passed Slough East at 2.51, braking with Dolphin's up main distant signal showing 'Caution' as the fast goods passed Langley on the down main. At 2.53 *Dudley Castle* came to a stand at Dolphin's up main home signals 40/46 as the fast goods passed on the down main line, as the 1.30 Old Oak Common passed Langley on the down relief and as the crawling Government Stores train cleared Langley on the up main. Bells and bell tappers clattered and jangled all along the darkened instrument shelf in Dolphin Junction. Now was the moment of decision – Welch could allow the express to follow the freight up the main line or he could switch it to the up relief line 'across the bows', so to speak, of the oncoming 1.30 a.m. Old Oak Common. Levers crashed and thudded as he threw the down relief line signals to 'Danger', reversed points A/B – but not C – and lowered signal 40. Welch reasoned that the 1.30 Old Oak Common had only just passed Langley, the driver would not only see the distant go back to amber – 'Caution' – he would also get the 'Caution' siren off the ATC. The Old Oak would easily be able to pull up, the Plymouth would be all right.

Sadly for several people the engine of the 1.30 a.m. Old Oak Common was not fitted with the GWR's ATC – it was a LMS engine on loan, a 2–8–0 No 8239. On its footplate, Driver Clay saw Dolphin's distant signal showing green and then turned inboard to find a spanner to tighten a leaky pipe joint. He never saw the signal go back to 'Caution'. Welch maintained that he never lowered the signals on the down relief line and that Driver Clay mistook Dolphin's down main distant for his own on the down relief, the two were side by side though separated by about 40 ft. The Inquiry gave Clay the benefit of the doubt for it seemed very unlikely that he could have mistaken another train's signal when that train had just rattled past him on the other line. Welch forgot to allow time for *Dudley Castle* to re-start – the official time, given in the working time-table, was two minutes which was a large part of the running time for the 1.30 a.m. Old Oak Common from Langley to Dolphin. He forgot to reverse point C and then, to crown everything, he had allowed a conflicting movement across the bows of the still moving, as yet out of sight, goods train.

Driver Clay saw the red lights of signal 11/4 through the arch of a bridge when he was 400 yds away and braked hard; 650 tons piled up behind the tender of his engine and drove it forward, a total of 757 tons, into the slowly advancing *Dudley Castle*. The left-hand buffer of 8239 struck *Dudley Castle*'s buffer beam dead centre where it was encroaching on the down relief line track and the force involved was such that the passenger train, weighing 365 tons was instantly reversed 12 ft. The second coach telescoped through the leading coach and both were crushed against the reversing engine. The tender of 8239 was wrenched from its massive coupling with the engine and was raised 25 ft by the goods trucks crushing in from behind. Both engines were shattered, five people were killed, five more were seriously injured – all because a conscientious signalman did not want to delay an express train.

The build-up of Allied military force through 1943–4 brought heavy work for the Great Western. The vast American armies needed new camps, airfield and ammunition dumps, the construction and supply of marshalling yards – built to some extent by Italian prisoners – and new signal boxes. The Didcot to Winchester line was doubled between Didcot and Newbury and modernised throughout to form a vital strategic route from the Midlands to Southampton docks. The old M&SW section came into its own once more serving camps old and new and a new ammunition depot was built on the southern edge of Savernake Forest, connected by a siding with the single track M&SW between Marlborough tunnel and Savernake High Level station, the entire set-up being known as North Savernake sidings to confuse spies. In 1944 a wooden truck carrying ammunition arrived at the siding with an over-heated axle-bearing blazing fiercely as red-hot metal ignited lubricating oil. The truck was shunted in, off the 'main line', the token was then restored to its instrument allowing another to be withdrawn to permit the 3.50 p.m. Marlborough to Andover 'school train' to leave Marlborough. The train, manned by Southern Railway crew, passed the siding just as the truck of ammunition exploded. Details of the event are at present hard to discover.

The Americans were a source of constant revelation – and chewing gum – to the British. Harry Keen booked on at Oxford to 'travel passenger' down to Brize Norton on the Fairford line to work a military special. The train was waiting for him at the platform and he was just opening a door to get in when he was brought up short by a fat soldier with white webbing belt and a white helmet. 'Just where the hell d'yuh think yore goin', Bub?' The question was emphasised by a big, black, Colt .45 automatic which the man held in his porky fist. It was pointed straight at Harry's eyes and the barrel seemed very, very wide. Harry jumped back onto the platform pretty damn quick and conducted negotiations through the window. 'I am the guard of this train, I want to board it.'

'I guess we ain't in need of no guards, Bub,' said the man, motioning left and right with his pistol. At each end of the corridor stood an equally heavy-looking Military Policeman each holding an ugly Colt automatic. The men in the compartments Harry then realised were prisoners, a train-load of them, tough and looking most resentful. Harry finally managed to get aboard his train and was rather glad that the MPs were there. 'I'd never have managed that lot of my own,' he said. 'Now that's what I really call guarding a train.'

With fewer forays over England by the Luftwaffe it seemed as if Allied planes were trying to make up the crash figures. Bombers used to over-run the runway at Brize Norton and came to rest on their nose on the Fairford branch. Training planes from White Waltham were known to impale themselves on the cast-iron, decorative spikes of GWR signals, and when the Americans arrived they certainly added to the fun. On 19 January 1944, a Lockheed Lightning from 22 Photographic Squadron, USAAF, was taking rather too close a look at High Wycombe and crashed into the station goods yard, close to High Wycombe Middle box. Signalman Day rushed down the steps to help and was joined by the men from the station and goods shed but it was not possible to get near the plane for flames and the unfortunate pilot, with the splendidly American name Wendell Blickendorfer, was burned alive.

Five days later, at Aldermaston, 5005 *Manorbier Castle* was standing at the head of the 8.20 a.m. Paddington – the 'Staff Train', which daily brought headquarters staff down to the 'evacuated' offices of the Company. While the train was emptying and crowds were streaming through the ticket gate into the station yard there came the terrific, snarling crescendo of a diving aircraft, followed by the insane, rapid batter of eight machine-guns. The confusion was absolute. Dozens stood rigid, petrified, scores threw themselves flat, more tried to run as the plane pulled out of its 400 mph dive and screamed away. Hundreds were shouting, arguing with each other, lady clerks were crying through it all. Men were saying, 'It was a Jerry suicide mission.' 'No! I tell you it was a Spitfire – a Spit with American markings.' And so it was. The only damage done was twelve bullet holes through 5005's tender. Normally the engine took the empty coaches to Newbury Race Course sidings to stable until required in the evening but now the engine was uncoupled and, with its tender spouting water like a collander, dashed away to the sidings where its fire was thrown out.

The perpetrator was a remarkably good shot for he opened fire at just the right distance to make the bullets converge on the tender, if the engine's boiler had been punctured there would have been a different tale to tell. His name nor his motive were ever disclosed but the record does state that he was given a 'severe reprimand' for his escapade.

The 109-years-old Company, loyal and dignified as an aged butler in the service of some great household, had suffered many indignities – grimy engines, a 500-kg bomb exploding in Paddington station*, restaurant cars forced to serve whalemeat instead of roast lamb – but the Aldermaston incident was the final humiliation. It would not have been quite so bad if it had been an American Mustang that shot up their train – but a *Spitfire* piloted by a Yank – Heavens!

In 1945, when the war was over, a Labour government was elected to bring about Labour's long-advocated, centrally planned, economy. Coal, gas, electricity, iron and steel, road and rail transport were to become public property. A gentleman from the Co-op, Alfred Barnes, was put in charge of the arrangements regarding the nationalisation of all transport and the date was set for the abolition of the Great Western Railway: midnight, 31 December 1947.

There was some restoration of pre-war services in 1945 including the re-introduction of slip coaches. A train with one slip coach had a pair of tail lamps side by side, one distinguished by a big red disc around the red lamp, the other with a big white disc around the white light, while the main train

* On platforms 6 & 7 at 1.05 a.m., 22 March 1944.

carried a pair of double red lamps one above the other. The men had to remember their time-table and know what sort of tail lamp to look for on various trains and after six years without slip coaches they were out of practice. In November 1945 an up express with a 'slip' for Didcot lost it at Knighton crossing, 16 miles short of its destination, because the guard unlocked the release lever and pulled it for some reason best known to himself. Instead of allowing his coach to run on to Uffington and get within the protection of fixed signals he braked and came to a stand out of sight of either signalman. This would not have mattered but the signalman at Uffington, who had never worked with slip coaches, seeing the tall, double red tail lamp of the main train, forgot that there ought to have been a 'slip' tail lamp showing and gave 'Train out of Section' to Knighton. Knighton then 'asked the road' for an up stopping passenger train. All would have been well if the signalman at Challow had noticed that the slip tail lamp was missing but he 'cleared back' and the stopping train came galloping along towards Knighton with all the 'boards' off and the slip coach, unprotected by its guard standing on the track. Luckily for all concerned the permanent-way men, who had been staring, puzzled at the lonely-looking slip coach, heard the stopping train coming, ran hard towards it, waving their arms and the splendid 'King' class engine, just out of the factory on a 'running-in' turn, managed to stop short of the coach. The alarm was raised in the signal boxes when George Strong, at Circourt, looking out especially to wave to his brother, the slip guard, saw what was missing and sent 5–5 on the bell 'Train Divided' to Wantage Road and 4–5 'Train passed without Tail Lamp' to Challow. There were some red faces but the stalwart permanent-way men each got 10s 6d and a certificate from a very grateful Great Western.

The year 1947 started very badly, there was a severe coal shortage and the worst winter for fifty years. Trains had to be cancelled; bitter weather and deep snow froze trains every-where; and in the hills of Wales and Devon trains were snowed

in for weeks. To get to trains stranded at Dowlais the Great
Western brought in two Rolls-Royce Derwent jet engines,
mounted on rail, operated by RAF personnel. When the trucks
were well chained down the engines were turned on. Everything disappeared in an indescribable din and positive wall of
ice. The deep snow had compacted and the jets ripped up slabs
of ice 6 ft long and 3 ft wide, flinging them for yards in all
directions. The experiment was very promptly abandoned.
England was dark, cold, and frequently candle-lit, for there
were frequent power cuts. Whalemeat was still being served in
restaurant cars eighteen months after the end of the war – and
then came the thaw. Roast beef was announced with a theatric-
al flourish by the Chief Steward of a Great Western dining car
to his crew of incredulous passengers. After the thaw came the
floods which washed away parts of the line and after the floods a
glorious summer which brought the Great British Public in
hordes to the major stations where they confidently expected to
find trains to bear them away to the 'Shire of the Sea Kings' as
in the days of old. Unfortunately for their dreams, the Great
Western was short of men, motive power – and coal. The
demand for transport simply could not be met and at Paddington vast queues were normal. Indeed, it was the Age of the
Queue. One queued for everything from two ounces of cheese to
trains, at holiday times in particular the 'Lawn' at Paddington
was jammed with humanity from ticket barriers to the GWR
Royal Hotel and the queue went off, six abreast, out of the
station, on both sides of the road, stretching down Eastbourne
Terrace for a mile!

The last Royal train on the Great Western took King George
VI and Queen Elizabeth (the present Queen Mother) to
Kingswear and back over 28/30 October as a similar train had
done for King Edward VII at the start of building the naval
college at Dartmouth in 1902, just as a very different train had
taken the young Queen Victoria from Windsor to Paddington
105 years before. The last public train on the Great Western
from Paddington left without ceremony. At 11.45 p.m., the

platforms were shiny black, wet with rain driven icily by a cruel little breeze. A small crowd of men stood on the platform ends, their attention focused on two grimy trains hauled by two grimy 'Castles', the Company's insignia only half visible on their tenders. At 11.50 p.m., the guard of the 11.50 p.m. to Plymouth raised his green light over his head, blew his pea-whistle and 5037 *Monmouth Castle* stepped into the rain-swept night. Not a 'shot' was fired, not a cheer was raised, as the last Great Western train left Paddington. The gun-crack Swindon exhaust was sufficient music, a stately drum-beat, slow and solemn at befited the funeral train of a heroic enterprise, which had so faithfully served England and Wales through the best and worst of 112 years of history.

EPILOGUE

At 12.5 a.m. on January 1948, 5032 *Usk Castle* took the first British Railways Western Region train out of Paddington to the sound of some scattered cheers and the sharp, flash-bang, of exploding fog signals. It was a muted welcome to the new regime, both engines were grimy, both had the noble old letters GWR on their tenders. Nothing much had changed. The Great Western had been a family affair, father to son often for generations, some families could tally 450 years' service between them and no doctrinaire legislation was going to change their feelings overnight. There were few who did not feel sad at the passing of the old firm and many were the private resolutions made to carry the old spirit of the Compamy into the new, Socialist world.

At the top of the Company tree feelings of hurt and disappointment were strong even though the change had been seen coming for some time. Sir James Milne, the last General Manager, a very brilliant man and Chairman of the wartime Railway Executive Committee, refused to become Chairman of a permanent Executive under the British Transport Commission sitting at Hotel Great Central in Marylebone Road – otherwise known as 'The Kremlin' – and most of the other senior Great Western Officers followed their Chief's example. Allan Quartermaine, Chief Engineer of the GWR, refused the equivalent post in the Executive when it was offered and F.W. Hawksworth, sixth and last occupant of the Chair of Daniel Gooch at Swindon, indignantly refused to shake hands with the new Chief Mechanical Engineer of British Railways, R.A. Riddles.

At the next level of Management, Milne's Assistant, Keith

Grand, took over the General Managership of Western Region and Gilbert Matthews, the last man to hold the hallowed title of Superintendent of the Line, a post instituted in 1838, became Chief Operating Officer, Western Region. With Great Western men still in charge at Paddington the directives emanating from 'The Kremlin' could be successfully resisted – which saved a lot of money – and, with a large proportion of the staff virtually hereditary Great Western employees, the old feelings of 'Pride in the Job' and service to the community continued to glow bright in the ashes of post-war Britain.

Felix Pole, the son of the village schoolmaster of Great Bedwyn, had joined the Great Western in 1891 as a fourteen-year-old messenger boy in Swindon telegraph office where he learned to use the single-needle telegraph instrument by ear – without watching the needle flicking left and right – and in a long lifetime never lost that skill, as he could demonstrate. He became General Manager of the Great Western in 1921, was knighted in 1924 and in 1929 resigned to become Chairman of Associated Electrical Industries. He retired from AEI in 1945, owing to the onset of blindness and went to live at Calcot Grange, near Reading, where the south-facing windows over-looked the Plymouth line. By 1951 he was totally blind but his affection for the Great Western, masquerading as Western Region, never dimmed nor did the men forget him. In 1953, a schoolboy railway enthusiast, David Blagrove, arranged an interview with him and was received with great charm, without any of the condescension Blagrove had half expected. Sir Felix told him that when he travelled from Great Bedwyn to Swindon to be interviewed for his job, the quickest route would have been via Savernake and Marlborough, over the M&SW, but he did not want to arrive for an interview on the Great Western with a 'foreign' railway company's ticket in his pocket so he took the longer, dearer route via Newbury, Compton and Didcot. After he had been taken on at Swindon he was travelling to work on the train and his father was with him. As they curved away from the main line at Newbury, to head north over the Berkshire downs, they passed Newbury East Junction signal box. Young Felix waved to the signalman who duly waved back. 'You haven't got to know that man already?' asked his father.

'No,' replied Felix, 'but we're friends, we work for the same concern.'

At 11 a.m. Sir Felix took Blagrove to stand by the tall windows. Soon they heard the whistle of a down train. 'Good men,' smiled Pole, 'they're warning me to get ready.' The whistle called again, Sir Felix began to wave and into sight, broadside on at the bottom of the garden, came the 'Cornish Riviera' with the driver and fireman waving for all they were worth. The old blind man, who had left the Great Western twenty-four years before, waved until the sound of the hurrying wheels died away. That was the spirit, the bond between Great Western men, which kept the job going through thick and thin and which transcended all legislation.

Bristol Divisional Superintendent's Report on the Great Storm, 28 March 1916

'At 1 a.m. today I had advice that the storm was still raging from Chipping Sodbury to Pilning and had brought the [telegraph] wires down at Patchway, cutting our communications with Severn Tunnel Junction except by the Holesmouth Junction to Pilning circuit and via this wire were able to ascertain that the 7.30 and 8.10 a.m. Bristol to Cardiff passengers would be accepted and were allowed to leave. At 9.7 a.m. the 10.57 p.m. [27 March] Cardiff arrived at Bristol [due at midnight] and Guard Morgan informed me that all the wires were down from Cardiff to Severn Tunnel Junction. He also said that his train had not arrived at Newport until 1.42 a.m. and had been hung up behind the 6.30 p.m. Neyland until 7.47 a.m. Knowing that trains could pass as far as Cardiff we allowed the 9.3 a.m. train to the North to leave though we had no information on the state of the line north of Maindee Junction (Newport), the examining light engine and Inspector not having been heard of since he left Newport for Pontypool Road at 4.35 a.m. [This engine was stuck in a snowdrift blocking the northbound line and preventing the 9.3 a.m. Bristol from passing. The 9.3 came to a stand at Maindee and thus blocked the down main line into Newport station.] The 12.40 a.m. Bristol–Manchester was routed over the Midland companies line which was unobstructed though all wires on that route were down.'

The Working of the 6.30 p.m. Neyland to Paddington Passenger and Mail Train: detail taken from Guard Campion's Journal, 27 March 1916

Make-up of the 6-30 pm Neyland–Paddington working, 27 March 1916

Train 1

BK 3RD	3RD	1ST–3RD	MILK	BRAKE VAN	SLEEPER	3RD	1ST–3RD	3RD	PARCELS	SIPHON	GPO	GPO
2813	1910	7257	1818	1106	7595	3626	7409	3606	829	1594	843	846

Locos: GWR ST.ANTHONY 3303 — ST.AUBYN 3355

Train 2

MILK	BRAKE VAN	SLEEPER	3RD	1ST–3RD	3RD	PARCELS	SIPHON	GPO	GPO
1818	1106	7595	3626	7409	3606	829	1594	843	846

Locos: GWR ST.ANTHONY 3303 — ST.AUBYN 3355

Train 3

MILK	BRAKE VAN	3RD	1ST–3RD	SIPHON	SIPHON	SIPHON	GPO	GPO
1818	1106	3626	7409	1594	868	784	843	846

Loco: 3813 CITY of CARMARTHEN

Train 4

BRAKE VAN	SLEEPER	3RD	1ST–3RD	3RD	PARCELS	SIPHON	3RD	SIPHON	SIPHON
1106	7595	3626	7409	3606	829	1594	7104	868	784

Loco: 3813 CITY of CARMARTHEN

MAKE–UP
1. NEYLAND – WHITLAND
2. WHITLAND – CARDIFF
3. CARDIFF – GLOUCESTER
4. GLOUCESTER – PADDINGTON*

MAKE UP OF THE 6-30 PM NEYLAND–PADDINGTON WORKING, 27 MARCH 1916, FROM GUARD CAMPION'S JOURNAL

*3813 changed for 2973 at Swindon

© Aw. 1985. R.D. CARTER.

Departed Neyland 6.30 p.m. Weather: Full Gale. Head Guard Campion, Junior Guard Shelley both of Paddington. Driver Thomas of Neyland with 3303 *St Anthony*, 3355 *St Aubyn* assisting. 10 1st class and 170 3rd class passengers for Paddington, 9 1st and 211 3rd class passengers for Cardiff.

Clynderwen 7.17–7.20 p.m. 1 minute late. Attach six-wheel milk van 1818 rear.

Whitland. 7.31–7.43 p.m. 1 minute late/5 minutes late. Attach three eight-wheel carriages, Pembroke to Salthouses.

St Clears. 7.53–7.54. 5 minutes late.

Carmarthen Jcn. 8.8–8.14 p.m. 5 minutes late

Llanelli. 8.38–8.45 p.m. 3 minutes late arriving. 5 minutes late leaving due to heavy parcel traffic.

Cockett summit passed 9.2 p.m. 5 minutes late.

Landore. 9.7–9.15 p.m. 4 minutes late arriving, 5 minutes late leaving due to heavy parcel traffic.

Swansea Valley Jcn. 9.18–9.21 p.m. at signals. 6 minutes running time lost.

Neath. 9.33–9.37 p.m. 11 minutes late.

Margam East box signal delay 3 minutes.

Bridgend. 10.12–10.17 p.m. 14 minutes late.

Signal delays at Miskin Crossing. Duffryn Bridge, Peterson West and East Cardiff. 11.9–11.21 p.m. 22 minutes lost to signals. 2 minutes lost attaching and detaching traffic. 38 minutes late from Cardiff.

Signal delays at Cardiff East, Longdyke, Pengam, Rhymney Bridge, St Mellons and Marshfield. 20 minutes lost.

Newport. 11.58 p.m. Unable to proceed.

Newport. Departed 7.35 a.m. 28 March. Head Guard Peckett, Junior Guard Davis of Newport. Fresh engine 3813 *County of Carmarthen*, Driver Mitchell of Swindon. Proceeded under Time Interval Working from Newport to Chepstow. Chepstow. 8.40–8.53 a.m. 1 minute lost drawing up to platform. 562 minutes late leaving. Time Interval Working Awre Jcn. to Newnham.

Gloucester. 9.54–10.18 a.m. Attaching and detaching. 593 minutes late.

Stroud. 10.35–10.38 a.m. 592 minutes late.

Brimscombe. 10.44–10.47 a.m. Special stop in place of 9.30 a.m. Gloucester. Attached bank engine in front. No 3118.

Time Interval Working Frampton Mansell to Sapperton.

Signal delay at Coates. 3 minutes lost.

Kemble. 11.10–11.15 a.m. 1 minute lost drawing up to platform. 598 minutes late.

Signal delay at Minety.

Swindon. 11.36–11.50 a.m. Waiting for a fresh engine, 7 minutes delay. 608 minutes late leaving. 2973 *Robins Bolitho*, Driver Pocock of Swindon.

Didcot. 12.23–12.26 p.m. 608 minutes late arriving, 609 late leaving. Reading. 12.47–12.54 p.m. 608 minutes late arriving, 609 late leaving.

Slough passed at 1.15 p.m. 607 minutes late.

Paddington. 1.34. Late arrival of 607 minutes.

Notes on the Locomotives

3303 *St Anthony* and 3355 *St Aubyn* both of the 4–4–0 type with the main frames placed outside the driving wheels. Two cylinders, placed inside the frames, 18 in. diameter by 30 in. stroke. Firegrate area, 21½ sq ft. Boiler pressure 180 lb psi. Diameter of driving wheels 5 ft 8 in. Weight of engine 59¾ tons, weight of tender 34 tons. 3303 built June 1906, 3355 built November 1900. 'Bulldog' class.

3813 *County of Carmarthen.* 4–4–0 type with driving wheels outside the main frames. Two cylinders, placed outside the frames, 18 in. diameter by 30 in. stroke. Firegrate area, 20½ sq ft. Boiler pressure 200 lb psi. Diameter of driving wheels 6 ft 8½ in. Weight of engine 55¼ tons, weight of tender 36¾ tons. Built November 1906. 'County' class.

2973 *Robins Bolitho.* 4–6–0 type, driving wheels outside the main frames, two cylinders, placed outside the frames, 18 in. diameter by 30 in. stroke. Firegrate area 27¾ sq ft. Boiler pressure 200 lb spi. Diameter of driving wheels 6 ft 8½ in. Weight of engine 67¾ tons, weight of tender 43 tons. Built March 1905. 'Saint' class.

Appendix 1

Notes on the vehicles forming the 6.30 p.m. Neyland

NUMBER	REMARKS
1106	Passenger brake van: 40 ft long, low roof, non-corridor connected. Built 1899.
7595	Sleeping car: 50 ft long, clerestory roof, composite class. Built 1805.
3606/3626	Carriages: 70 ft long, high roof, 'Concertina' types. Built 1906/7.
7409	Carriage: clerestory roof, four lavatories, one at each end and two together centrally. 1st/3rd class seating. Built 1897.
1910	Carriage: 46 ft long, clerestory roof, non-corridor. Built 1890.
2813	Passenger brake van/3rd class carriage. Built 1900.
7257	Passenger brake van/1st and 3rd class carriage: 56 ft long non-corridor. A 'Falmouth coupé' with observation window at one end. Built 1894.
1594	Designated officially as a 'fish van': 70 ft long, high roof, air and vacuum brakes, corridor connected. Built 1903.
829	Parcels van: 70 ft long, high roof, corridor connected. Built 1905. ·
868	News van: 47 ft 6 in. long, low roof, side corridor connections for use with the GPO's Travelling Post Office vehicles. Built 1900.
784	News van: 40 ft long, low roof, non-corridor connected. Built 1889.
843	Travelling Post Office van: 46 ft 6 in. long, clerestory roof, side corridor connections. Used to sort letters en route, fitted with nets to pick up mail bags and arms to set down mail bags at speed. Built December 1884.
846	Travelling Post Office, as above: Built November 1894.
1818	Van: six-wheeled, low roof. Built *c.* 1880.

APPENDIX TWO

Severn Tunnel Bank Engines

Hours of Duty, 1929

No.		Men change at
1	12 midnight – 4 p.m.	8 a.m.
2	1 a.m. – 5 p.m.	- - -
3	2 a.m. – 6 p.m.	10 a.m.
4	4 a.m. – 12 noon MO	- - -
5	9 a.m. – 5 p.m.	- - -
6	12 noon – 4 a.m.	8 p.m.
7	3.20 p.m. – 7.20 a.m.	11.20 p.m.
8	5 p.m. – 9 a.m.	1 a.m.
9	6.30 p.m. – 10.30 a.m.	2.30 a.m.
10	7.30 p.m. – 11.30 a.m.	3.30 a.m.

All bank engines to go to shed as soon as possible on Sunday mornings. The times given are those at which the Engines start and finish at Severn Tunnel Junction.

Estimated cost of providing accommodation for steam and electric locomotives at Taunton. Information given at Paddington, 11 October 1938

SCHEME 1. To retain existing steam engine shed and to build a new shed for electric locomotives on the downside of the line at 163¾ mile post. Up electric locos to come off train at electric loco shed and steam engine from existing steam shed to take train on to Taunton station. Down steam locos to come off train at Taunton station and to go on to steam shed. Electric locos to come from electric loco shed.

    Reqd. No. of electric locos?   No. of steam locos?

    Estimated cost of electric locos shed with site

    Estimated cost of signalling arrangements

    Traffic department opinion re: stopping in section to change engines and occupation of lines. Traffic department to provide estimate of signalling arrangements.

Total cost of shed, land, signals – shed will accommodate 18 electric locos: £52,800

SCHEME 2. Abandon existing steam engine shed, provide new shed for steam and electric locos at 164¼ mile post. Electric loco shed will accommodate 18 and steam side of shed will accommodate 22 locomotives.

Total cost of shed, signals, land: £145,700

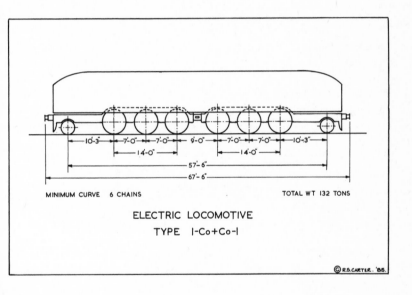

MINIMUM CURVE   6 CHAINS   TOTAL WT 132 TONS

ELECTRIC LOCOMOTIVE
TYPE   1-Co+Co-1

© R.S.CARTER. '85.

Estimated cost of providing accommodation for electric locomotives only

SCHEME I	£
Land, 6 acres at £200 per acre	1200
Filling-in and excavating 36,000 cu. yds	4500
Shed for electric locos. (220 ft × 97 ft 6 in. × 25ft 6 in. average height, and offices (220 ft × 10 ft × 15 ft 6 in.)	21000
Sand-drier house and drier	500
Boilerhouse and one boiler	900
Repair shop	2500
Turnouts 17 off	3400
Diamond crossings 2 off	440
Stop blocks 3 off	120
Wheel stops 6 sets	18
Catch points 1 off	25
Pits 1200 ft	4800
Sidings 1866 yds	4200
Lighting of shed and yard	850
Heating of shed	350
Vacuum oil tanks, furniture for offices and messrooms	1000
Water tank – second-hand – 13 ft 6 in. × 13 ft 6 in. × 4 ft 9 in. including sealed cover, erected on convenient building.	300
Water mains, 2 in., 1200 ft	210
Sundry water appliances	150
Hydrants	70
Allow for boundary fences	500
Allow for machinery and tools for light repairs	1500
Contingencies	5167
	53,700

NB: Estimate for signal department work not included, say £1800

Total cost estimated   £55,500

Initialled: CBM

Estimated cost of providing accommodation for electric and steam locomotives

SCHEME 2   £

Land, 18½ acres at £200 per acre	3700
Filling in and excavating site 106,000 cu. yds	16,200
Engine shed (220 ft × 203 ft × 25 ft 6 in. average height) and offices (220 ft × 16 ft × 15 ft 6 in. average height)	42,000
Coal stage (44 ft × 36 ft) with elevated road (tank included in water appliances)	3600
Sand-drier house and two driers	500
Boiler washing plant with 2 boilers and houses	2400
Turnouts 33 off	6600
Diamond crossings 3 off	660
Stop blocks 10 off	400
Wheel stops 11 sets	40
Single compound 1 off	300
Sidings 4960 yds	11,160
Pits 2940 ft	11,760
Catch points 2 sets	50
Turntable, 70 ft complete with foundations	4000
Lighting of shed and yard	1350
Heating of shed for electric locos	600
Vacuum oil tanks and furniture for offices and messrooms	2000
Water tank on coal stage, water mains and appliances	5350
Allow for boundary fences	1000
Contingencies	10,030
NB Estimate for signal department not included but believed	7000
Total cost, say	£ 130,700

Initialled: CBM

APPENDIX FOUR

Great Western's role
in the Evacuation of Dunkirk, 1940

Mr Winston Churchill stated in Parliament that the operation of the evacuation was 'A miracle of deliverance, achieved by valour, by perseverance, by perfect discipline, by faultless service, by resource, by skill, by unconquerable fidelity which is manifest to us all.'

At the time of the Dunkirk evacuation the railways were called on to provide carriages and motive power at a moment's notice not only for the returning soldiers but for troop movements within Britain and for the evacuation of civilians from likely invasion zones in Kent and East Anglia. The Great Western took almost all the Dunkirk evacuation trains and many others too.

	Dunkirk evac. trains	Total no of men	Av. no per train	No of other troop trains
29 May	21	10,787	514	16
30 "	42	21,817	519	21
31 "	76	70,054	922	22
1 June	79	41,492	525	16
2 "	29	15,392	531	17
3 "	14	7,360	526	16
4 "	32	15,613	488	33
	293	182,515	575	141

Besides these, the Great Western, during the same period handled 31 specials of evacuated men, women and children making the total number of special trains from 29 May to 4 June 465 and the total number of people carried 205,087. The Minister of Transport wrote to thank the General Manager of the Great Western, Sir James Milne;

part of the letter saying 'To organise and carry through without a
hitch an operation of this magnitude is an achievement of which you
may be justly proud.' Milne wrote to many of the men, who had taken
part in the Great Western's land and sea rescue operation, to thank
them, and the reply to him from one of them sums up the spirit of the
country and of the Great Western: 'In view of the superhuman efforts
of our retiring troops and the courageous men who covered the
evacuation it would have been a sad thing if the Great Western had
failed to do its part. I can assure you, sir, that every railwayman of
every grade, who had the honour to share in this great event, were,
one and all, determined that every demand made upon them and the
railway should be adequately and efficiently met.'

The Great Western's Navy in 1939

	Put in Service	Gross Tonnage	Draught	Knots	Passenger Accommodation
St Andrew	Feb 1932	2702	14ft 3in.	21	1360
St David	March 1932	2702	14ft 3in.	21	1360
St Patrick	March 1930	1922	13ft 7in.	19	913
St Helier	June 1925	1952	13ft ½in.	18	1048
St Julien	May 1925	1952	13ft ½in.	18	1048
Roebuck	April 1925	776	12ft 6½in.	12¼	Nil
Sambur	May 1925	776	12ft 6½in.	12¼	Nil
Great Western	Jan 1934	1659	13ft 0in.	14	450
Sir Richard Grenville	July 1931	896	11ft 9½in.	13	801
Sir Walter Raleigh	April 1908	478	10ft 8in.	12	285
Sir Francis Drake	April 1908	478	10ft 8in.	13	555
Sir John Hawkins	July 1929	930	11ft 3in.	13	809
Mew	May 1908	117	6ft 0in.	10	543

St Andrew and *St David* were on the Fishguard–Rosslare run; *Great
Western* on the Fishguard–Waterford; *St Helier*, *St Julien* and *St Patrick*
plied between Weymouth and the Channel Islands with passengers
(*St Patrick* worked on the Irish run in the winters); *Roebuck* and *Sambur*
carried freight on that route. *Mew* was a ferry across the River Dart
between Dartmouth and Kingswear and the four 'Knights' were

tenders used to convey passengers from transatlantic liners which anchored outside the breakwater at Plymouth and the 'Ocean Liner' expresses drawn up on the quay at Millbay Dock station. These four ships were taken over by the Royal Navy for use as 'Examination vessels' in the Plymouth area, *Sir Richard Grenville, Sir Walter Raleigh* and *Sir Francis Drake* on 25 August 1939 and *Sir John Hawkins* on 27 August 1940. *Mew*, whose shallow draught and relatively high carrying capacity made her an ideal vessel to take troops right off the beaches out to the bigger ships, was requisitioned for the Dunkirk evacuation on 30 May 1940. Her crew immediately provisioned the vessel and sailed their cross-river ferry up the Channel to Dover, leaving Dartmouth at 6 a.m. on the 31st. By that time the Dunkirk evacuation was almost complete and *Mew* was ordered back to Dartmouth. A tabular history of the wartime career of the other ships is given below.

	Requisitioned	Remarks
St Helier	9/9/39	Troop ship. Dunkirk/St Valery 22/5 – 21/6/40
St Julien	9/9/39	Troop ship. Dunkirk 20/5 – 31/5/40
St Andrew	11/9/39	Hospital Ship. Dunkirk 20/5 – 31/5/40
St David	23/9/39	Hospital ship. Dunkirk 24/5 – 2/6/40
	Sunk by enemy bombing during the Anzio landings 24/1/44	
St. Patrick	30/9/39	Troop ship. Returned to Fishguard 11/10/39
	Sunk by enemy bombing between Waterford and Fishguard 13/6/41	
Roebuck	29/5/40	Troop ship. Dunkirk/St Valery 29/5 – 13/6/40
Sambur	9/6/40	Troop ship. St Valery only 9/6 – 13/6/40
Great Western	11/5/44	Troop ship. Until October 1944

Ships requisitioned for the duration of the war except as shown

APPENDIX FIVE

Resignation letter of the General Manager of the Great Western Railway, Sir James Milne, KCVO, CSI, to the Chairman of the Great Western Board, Viscount Portal

Dildawn
Woldingham
Surrey
21 August 1947

My Dear Chairman

For sometime past you have been aware of my desire to retire before our beloved Company is vested in the British Transport Commission and I am very sad at having now to write to you formally and place my resignation in your hands. I am very proud to have had the honour of serving the Board in my capacity of General Manager of the Compnay over 18 years and it is difficult for me to find any words which would convey my deep feelings of gratitude to you personally and to all other members of the Board for the unfailing courtesy, consideration and wonderful kindness I have received during my long term of office.

The knowledge that I enjoyed the confidence of the Board and the support given to me by you and former Chairmen made my work a pleasure and it is mainly due to the friendly relations which exist between the Directors and the Officers that a team spirit has been built up which is the envy of all other railway companies and without which we could not have hoped to maintain the traditions and high reputation of our great undertaking.

Thanking you personally for all you have done for me,
I am,
Yours very sincerely,
James Milne

INDEX